A COLLECTION OF PERFORMANCE TASKS AND RUBRICS: FOREIGN LANGUAGES

Deborah Blaz

EYE ON EDUCATION

6 DEPOT WAY WEST, SUITE 106

LARCHMONT, NY 10538

(914) 833–0551

(914) 833–0761 fax

www.eyeoneducation.com

For information about permission to reproduce selections from this book, write: Eye On Education, Permissions Dept., Suite 106, 6 Depot Way West, Larchmont, NY 10538.

Library of Congress Cataloging-in-Publication Data

Blaz, Deborah
    A collection of performance tasks and rubrics : foreign languages / by Deborah Blaz.
        p. cm.
    Includes bibliographical references.
    ISBN 1-930556-06-3
    1. Language and languages—Ability testing. 2. Language and languages—Examinations. I. Title.

P53.4.B59 2001

00-57655

10 9 8 7 6 5 4 3 2

Editorial and production services provided by
Richard H. Adin Freelance Editorial Services
52 Oakwood Blvd., Poughkeepsie, NY 12603-4112
(845-471-3566)

Also Available from EYE ON EDUCATION

**Foreign Language Teacher's
Guide to Active Learning**
by Deborah Blaz

Teaching Foreign Languages in the Block
by Deborah Blaz

**Performance Standards
and Authentic Learning**
by Allan A. Glatthorn

**Performance Assessment and
Standards Based Curricula:
The Achievement Cycle**
by Allan Glatthorn
with Don Bragaw, Karen Dawkins,
and John Parker

**Developing Parent and Community
Understanding of Performance-
Based Assessment**
by Kathryn Anderson Alvestad

**Personalized Instruction:
Changing Classroom Practice**
by James Keefe and John Jenkins

ABOUT THE AUTHOR

Deborah Blaz, a French teacher at Angola High School in Angola, Indiana, is a native of St. Charles, Illinois. She received her B.A. in French and German from Illinois State University, a *diplome* from the Université de Grenoble in Grenoble, France, and, in 1974, an M.A. in French from the University of Kentucky. Ms. Blaz has taught French and English to grades 7 through 12 for the past 20 years in Indiana.

Ms. Blaz is the author of two best selling reference books, *The Foreign Language Teacher's Guide to Active Learning* and *Teaching Foreign Languages in the Block*. She has frequently presented on successful teaching strategies at national conferences, universities, and high schools. A recipient of the Project E Excellence in Education award for the year 2000, she was also named Indiana's French Teacher of the Year by the Indiana chapter of the American Association of Teachers of French (IAATF) in 1998, and was named to the All-USA Teacher team, Honorable Mention, by USA Today in 1996.

She may be contacted at Angola High School, 755 100 E, Angola, IN 46703.

ACKNOWLEDGMENTS

I would like to thank the following educators for their valuable contributions to this collection of performance tasks and rubrics:

- Al Bode, Spanish teacher, Charles City High School, Charles City, IA

- Kate Bourque, Spanish and English teacher, Murdock Middle High School, Winchendon, MA

- Kathleen Sweeney Bulger, Spanish teacher, Cadillac High School, Cadillac, MI

- Kelly Ferguson, Spanish teacher, Pioneer Westfield High School, Westfield, WI

- Susan Gross, French teacher, Cheyenne Mountain Middle School, Colorado Springs, CO

- Sandra Howard, French teacher, Marin Catholic High School, Kentfield, CA

- Vernon E. Jacobs, Associate Superintendent, Glendale Union High School District, Glendale, AZ

- Kimberly Kaufman, Spanish teacher, Wellesley High School, Wellesley, MA and her fellow Classical and Modern Language Department members at Wellesley: Richard Deppe, Sue DiGiandomenico, Paul Esposito, Mary Gottschalk, Mim Grodberg, Peter Haggerty, Jim Kelleher, Christine Laborde-Castérot, Susan Moore, Lynn Moore-Benson, and Marlies Stueart

- Lynette Lang, French teacher, Hampshire High School, Hampshire, IL

- Rebecca Peters, French teacher, White Plains Middle School for the Humanities, Eastview, White Plains, NY

- Mary Young, French teacher, Norte Vista High School, Riverside, CA

I would also like to thank Jan Rowe and Greg Allen who reviewed this book in manuscript form, and my publisher, Bob Sickles.

TABLE OF CONTENTS

1

WHY USE PERFORMANCE ASSESSMENTS?

Clearly, assessment is a popular topic encountered in publications, workshops and inservices, college training courses, and discussions in the teacher's lunchroom. Why is there a sudden interest in assessment strategies? The interest in multiple intelligences, new research and discoveries on how the brain learns a language, and new technologies (such as the Internet) now available in many classrooms, have forced us to reevaluate and often to modify our teaching methods. Especially influential is the emphasis on relevance, which acknowledges the effect context has on performance, and which leads us to want assessment strategies that reflect this new emphasis.

The word "assess" comes from the Latin, meaning "to sit beside." Tutors sat beside their students, correcting, praising, or admonishing them, and guiding them toward a better performance. Modern teaching practices, supported by research on learning, are now trying to return to this concept of the teacher as a "guide by the side," and assessment must adapt to reflect this change as well.

The American Council on the Teaching of Foreign Languages and the National Standards in Foreign Education Project have, at long last, released the Standards for Foreign Language Learning. The many different language organizations, such as the American Association of Teachers of French (AATF), American Association of Teachers of Spanish and Portuguese (AATSP), and others are in the process of adapting those standards more specifically for the strengths and particular requirements of each language. However, teachers are still dependent on the textbook publishers or their own ingenuity when it comes to assessing the degree of knowledge and proficiency of their students. It is this need that this book addresses, first by discussing in Chapter 1 the need for variety in assessment, in Chapter 2 by exploring how to choose an evaluation based on curriculum and how to create a rubric for that assessment tool, and, finally, in the following chapters, by discussing methods of evaluation based on a student's performance in the four main areas of foreign languages: speaking, writing, reading, and listening.

This is not an "ivory tower" treatise on assessments. Each section includes actual "tried-and-true" assessments contributed by foreign language teachers from all over the United States as well as examples of student work and explanations of scoring of that work. It is hoped that each can be used or adapted immediately for your classroom, as well as serving as models for creation of additional tasks of your own.

WHAT IS AN ASSESSMENT?

Assessment may be defined as "any method used to better understand the current knowledge that a student possesses." This means that an assessment can be almost anything, from a teacher's subjective judgment based on a single observation of student performance to a five-hour standardized test. Assessment may affect decisions about placement in a certain level, grades, advancement to the next level of a language, instructional needs, and changes in teaching strategies or curriculum.

In many classrooms, the primary purpose of assessment is to determine a student's grade. Teachers tend to think of "assessment" as being synonymous and interchangeable with "testing," "grading" and "evaluation," and the main form of assessment used is a pencil-and-paper test. This is not to say that these tests are not appropriate, but just that, alone, they are not enough. The national commission, whose findings are published in *Breaking Ranks: Changing an American Institution* (NASSP, 1996), says that teachers should "assess the academic progress of students in a variety of ways so that a clear and valid picture emerges of what they know and are able to do" (p. 54).

What teachers, students, and parents need, therefore, are *multiple and varied forms* of assessments: performance assessments such as portfolios and journals, evaluations of student products, and traditional paper-and-pencil assessments. This rich mixture should do several things:

- ♦ It should tell what the student knows and how it relates to the curriculum.

- ♦ It should provide an opportunity for the student to demonstrate what they can do with what they have learned.

- ♦ It should provide a method for assessing the student's achievement as compared with that of other students.

- ♦ It should be rigorous, yet fair enough so that students know what is expected of them, and have confidence in their ability to accomplish the task.

♦ It should provide a rich supply of information that reflects student progress.

Mastering the basic principles of assessment is not easy. First, we need to know and carefully consider the following five standards of assessment (Stiggins, 1996):

♦ Standard 1: Quality assessment arises from and accurately reflects clearly specified and appropriate achievement expectations for students.

What is our target for this assessment? What skills must a student have mastered? We cannot select the proper assessment method without first considering what sort of performance is expected. First, look at the goals/outcomes in your curriculum. Then, choose a performance that illustrates achievement of that goal.

♦ Standard 2: Sound assessments are specifically designed to serve instructional purposes.

Who will use the results of this assessment, and how? Figure 1.1 lists the users for any given assessment, along with what information they need and what questions need to be answered. It should be obvious that each user has different informational needs, and so, before writing an assessment, we need to determine who will use this assessment.

♦ Standard 3: Quality assessments accurately reflect the intended target and serve the intended purpose.

We need to match the target with the correct assessment method, and to do this requires using a variety of methods as well as evaluating the assessment after it has been given. Chapter 2 discusses how to select an appropriate assessment and write a rubric for scoring that activity.

♦ Standard 4: Quality assessments provide a representative sample of student performance that is sufficient in its scope to permit confident conclusions about student achievement.

A fine balance must be achieved between having a representative sample of different activities and having a large enough sample to determine how a student would be able to handle any possible situation related to the topic. The smallest amount possible of necessary examples should be used so that students are not overly stressed,

FIGURE 1.1 USES AND USERS OF ASSESSMENT

User	Question(s)	Information necessary
Student	What are my teacher's values? What do I need to do to succeed? Are the results worth the effort?	Continuous information about student performance
Teacher	What sort of help do students need? Which students need help? What grade goes on the report card? Did my teaching strategies work? How do I improve my teaching?	Continuous information about student performance Continuous information about group performance
Parent	Is my child successful in school? What does my child need to succeed? Is the teacher doing a good job? Is the school doing a good job?	Continuous feedback on their child's mastery of material taught
Administrator	Is the teacher doing a good job? Is the necessary material being learned? Is our curriculum effective? What sort of professional development will help?	Periodic feedback on group performance
District	Does the assessment measure the program's desired outcomes? Is there a need for revision of curriculum? Is there a need for revision of assessment? What changes need to be made in instructional strategies?	Continuous feedback on curriculum assessment instruction for the entire district, resulting in improvement of the district and the school system.

and testing does not exceedingly monopolize class time. Chapter 7 discusses methods for streamlining and facilitating the use of performance assessments.

♦ Standard 5: Sound assessments are designed, developed, and used in such a manner as to eliminate sources of bias or distortion that interfere with the accuracy of the results.

Elements that cause distortion may come from the test, from students, or from the classroom environment. Examples of poor tests include those tests with poorly worded questions or questions that might include cultural bias, with questions that are incorrectly scored, or those whose length causes student discomfort (i.e., those that require them to sit for long periods with no breaks). A student may experience extreme test anxiety, misinterpret questions, cheat, guess, or just plain lack motivation to perform. The classroom may be poorly lighted, too cold or too warm, or be in some way noisy or distracting, such as having a fire drill or unannounced visitor.

INCORPORATING BRAIN RESEARCH INTO ASSESSMENT

Implementing these standards should also incorporate recent brain research. It is important to ensure that an assessment reflects *how* students learn as well as what they learn. We must make sure that our assessments reflect several critical aspects of the learning process:

♦ Location

Test students in the same location that the material was taught. If, on a nice day, you took them outside to do observations or to perform a skit, or if they sat on the floor to practice verb endings, then make sure they are assessed there as well. Episodic memory is location-driven and changing locations will hinder students' ability to access that memory as will the teacher's absence. Because your presence was part of the students' experience, having them tested by a substitute teacher will also influence their ability to remember material. If the handout was on a particular color of paper, have the test on that color as well.

♦ Mood

Your enthusiasm will connect with your students, during both the teaching of the material and the assessment. If you have been bubbly and enthusiastic, becoming stern and quiet during testing may affect students' performance. Make the assessment a cause for celebration by telling them how confident you are of their ability or congratulating them during an assessment for a correct response, just like you do during instruction.

♦ Movement

A type of memory called procedural memory is also known as "muscle memory." If you have taught material using movements, music, or other kinesthetic methods, encourage students to physically perform the signals, steps, and songs that will help them access that memory. (You will probably want to have them do this silently.) We have all had the experience of losing an object and, by retracing our steps and performing actions in the same sequence as before, found what was lost. Allowing students to move quietly about the room or gesture at their seats may be an integral part of accessing information learned in this way.

♦ Unannounced assessment

This may be the most controversial aspect, but according to brain research, if you review with students or allow them to review their notes just before a test, they will transfer the information into their working (formerly called short-term) memory just for a short period of time, and therefore, you will be assessing what they have in their working memory, rather than assessing what is in the long-term storage part of the brain (Sousa, 1995). Assessing students periodically without warning seems, therefore, to be a strategy that will reveal what students really know well.

HOW DO WE BEGIN?

To write good assessments requires the use of individual effort, teams to share insights through interaction and professional development, a commitment to experimentation, and a realization that assessment is not, and should not be, static. The first thing to do is identify the purpose of the assessment (see Figure 1.2).

The purposes listed in Figure 1.2 are applicable to students, teachers, and administrators. Assessments serve to monitor students' understanding or lack of it on a given unit or concept, giving valuable feedback to the students and their teacher on what progress has been made and what still needs to be mastered. An assessment would also help teachers with instructional decision-

---

FIGURE 1.2 PURPOSES OF ASSESSMENT

- ◆ Monitor progress

- ◆ Clarify expectations

- ◆ Motivate

- ◆ Educate

- ◆ Communicate outcomes

- ◆ Document results

- ◆ Evaluate content programs

---

making issues such as what strategies seem to work best, or even how to spend resources.

Assessments also clarify performance expectations. Who has not experienced the special apprehension of the first test taken in a new class, from a different instructor, trying to anticipate what sorts of information a teacher will value, and how it should best be displayed? Students learn from a test what ideas and skills a teacher values and what the performance expectations are (i.e., how much a wrong accent mark or a misspelling will count against them). When constructing an assessment, teachers need to review the concepts covered and decide what is truly important for a student to know in order to succeed, which questions are worth the most points, how they should be assessed, and also how to review this material before the assessment. Finally, teachers should always make sure assessments are aligned with the desired outcomes found in local, district, state, and/or national curriculum content.

Assessments, especially performance assessments, are used to motivate. Students are told they need to know material "for the test." Teachers' grades are often published, or at least compared from department to department, and if scores are too low, teachers can be evaluated and remediated where needed, or an investigation launched to determine the cause. A well-constructed performance assessment will additionally motivate a student because it will elicit a unique individualized response that is, hopefully, authentic, and perhaps even creative, and that will stimulate the student to produce a quality response. Authenticity is discussed in more detail later in this chapter.

Finally, an assessment is a valuable tool that can be used to communicate with the student, his or her parents, a supervisor, or the administration. A performance assessment is a visible manifestation of a student's proficiency or lack of it; a graphic example that can be shared with a student (or even be student-generated) to evaluate progress, or shared with a parent who asks about a student's performance. Assessment products may be displayed in the classroom, the hallway, or the newspaper, to advertise that learning takes place in a classroom.

WHEN SHOULD WE ASSESS?

A good assessment is not an end result of the instructional process, but an evaluation that could occur at the beginning, to test what a student already knows or remembers; at the middle, to evaluate how much progress has occurred; or at the end. In any case, an assessment provides feedback for the teacher, the student, or any other interested party, on how well things are going. It is a good idea to build some sort of assessment into every lesson plan, every day.

WHY USE A PERFORMANCE ASSESSMENT?

Virtually all teachers report improved quality of student work when they begin using performance assessment. This is due to several factors:

♦ Clarity

When students know exactly what is expected, they are more likely to be able to produce it.

♦ Confidence

When understanding the criteria for the assignment provides students with clear guidelines and due dates for their work, they are sure of doing the job correctly. This tends to increase student engagement, as well as pride in the end result.

♦ High expectations

A well-written rubric defines what an excellent product is and sends the powerful message that anyone can produce work of that quality by adhering to those standards.

♦ Student engagement

When a performance assessment is highly authentic, students are more motivated to do the assignment, and the quality of student work is generally high.

♦ Parent understanding

Performance assessments better document student proficiency (or lack of it). Performance assessments are invaluable for parent conferences or open houses, to validate the teacher's judgment, especially when a teacher is concerned about a student and needs to persuade a parent that action is needed. (This is also true for communications with guidance personnel or administrators.)

Recently, new mandates for performance-based and portfolio-based statewide testing began in Arizona, California, Connecticut, Kentucky, Maryland, and New York. Many researchers and experts on education criticize regular multiple-choice type tests, saying they are not effective in measuring communication skills, complex problem-solving skills, creative thinking, and collaborative efforts among students. For example, Resnick and Resnick (1989) state that standardized tests contain short, choppy, superficial reading passages, ask students to search for information in bits, or to passively recognize errors (rather than producing corrections), or to fill in preselected responses to other people's questions. Other sources cite that many tests encourage memorization rather than understanding, and reiterate that students are asked to select, rather than to construct, an answer. Active participation has a further advantage in that the students exhibit greater interest and levels of learning when they are required to organize facts around major concepts and actively construct their answer in a variety of contexts, which is what performance assessments are all about.

HOW DOES LEARNING TAKE PLACE DURING PERFORMANCE ASSESSMENT?

Mislevy (1989) observes that standard test theory is "incompatible" with recent discoveries in cognitive and educational psychology. The assessments we use are based upon our beliefs about how learning occurs. Earlier, it was accepted as truth that learning needed to be broken down into a series of smaller skills units; a sort of "building blocks" approach based on the assumption that, after rote learning of these basics, you could proceed on to more complex understanding of them. Evidence from contemporary cognitive psychology, however, now tells us that learning requires learners to actively think about and construct their own unique knowledge structures, which will evolve as further learning takes place. People are not viewed as mere recorders of information, but as reflective, self-regulated participants in the learning process. To know something, one has to not simply receive information, but also place it in a context and relate it to other knowledge.

Cognitive psychology has found that learning is not linear, but proceeds in multiple directions all at once, and at an uneven pace. Learning can occur even when all basic facts have not been mastered. People are constantly reviewing and refining their knowledge. Learners increase their competency, not by simply accumulating new facts and skills, but by reconfiguring their knowledge structures, by automating procedures and chunking information to reduce memory loads, and by developing strategies and models that tell them when and how facts and skills are relevant. Based on these findings, what should be emphasized in modern education is how and whether students organize, structure, and use information, which cannot be tested by traditional multiple-choice or matching tests.

This is especially applicable to foreign language learning, in which we recognize the importance of not just what to say or do, but also when to do this, and how to adapt this performance to new situations. Cognitive psychology tells us that instruction that strongly emphasizes structured drill and memorization of factual knowledge does students a major disservice. Students need to be taught ways to organize the information and make it easy to remember and apply it to real-world situations. Mere acquisition of knowledge does not mean mastery of communication; thinking skills and problem-solving strategies such as circumlocution also need to be learned, as well as when and how to use them. That is why the new national standards emphasize and define student performance goals, and that is what we should be testing, for the most part.

INCORPORATING MODERN STRATEGIES

The role of a social context has also been studied a lot in recent years. It seems that real-life problem solving often requires people to work as a group, yet most traditional assessments are done on an individual basis. Group learning occurs through modeling effective thinking strategies, providing constructive feedback, and constructing complicated performances.

Finally, ask yourself: Do I teach a foreign language the same way that I was taught or do I incorporate new techniques or strategies such as TPRS (Total Physical Response Storytelling) or the Internet? Perhaps your focus has changed due to the new national standards with their emphasis on using material in context, and performance is the emphasis now in your classroom. Critical to performance-based learning is performance-based assessment. For example, does it make good sense to ask a dancer to take a multiple-choice test to determine whether she knows how to perform the cha-cha? Innovative means of instruction call for innovative means of assessment. Most standardized achievement tests measure traditional basic skills and are not particularly effective in measuring the higher-order thinking skills that are crucial for the twenty-first century.

WHAT IS A PERFORMANCE ASSESSMENT?

Performance-based learning entails students doing something. It may be performing tasks such as:

♦ Conversing in a foreign language;

♦ Assembling a model;

♦ Writing a story;

♦ Conducting research;

♦ Using a map;

♦ Using software on the computer;

♦ Painting a mural; or

♦ Performing a dance.

The list goes on and on.

A performance assessment can be defined as any procedure that asks a student to create or construct an answer. Figure 1.3 illustrates some of the differences between a traditional assessment such as those provided by a textbook series, and a performance assessment.

The best performance assessments have many, but not necessarily all, of the qualities listed in Figure 1.3. In a nutshell, performance assessments require a student to show us what they know and what they can do, in a meaningful, real-world application that is based on the curriculum's listed "student outcomes." Students know in advance what the criteria for their performance are, and often have input in deciding what those will be. These assessments are scored on a point scale based on well-defined criteria (a rubric) that is also presented in advance. Performance assessment requires students to be active participants who are learning even while they are being assessed.

A good example that contrasts a performance assessment with a regular test is the constructed-response answer. In a regular test, students routinely select from an array of possible answers, for example, a listening selection that asks a question, and students select the "best" answer from three or four possibilities. In a constructed-response questions the student, with the same prompt, is required to produce his or her own answer. A constructed-response question may have just one correct answer, or it may be more open ended, allowing a range of responses. The form can also vary, ranging from filling in a blank or writing a short answer to drawing a picture of what took place, indicating their agreement or disagreement with the speaker on a graph or diagram, or writing out all the steps in making a piñata.

FIGURE 1.3 TRADITIONAL ASSESSMENTS VS. PERFORMANCE ASSESSMENTS

Characteristics: paper/pencil, true/false, matching, multiple choice	*Characteristics:* not necessarily written, constructed response required
Objective	More than one correct answer
Hard to write	Time-consuming to set up
Easy to grade/machine-scored	Rubric-scored
Testing for validity, group norms	Individualized response
Isolated application	Contextualized, authentic application ("meaningful")
Facts, memorized data and procedures	Metacognitive, complex behaviors such as collaborative skills and intrapersonal skills
Items not interconnected, related	Integrated, possibly even cross-disciplinary
Lower-level thinking skills	Reasoning, problem solving, collaborative effort
Answering options provided (student passive)	Individualized response (student active)
Provided by text or teacher-constructed	Student involvement in setting goals and criteria
Standards determined/discovered after test to assure confidentiality	Published standards known in advance
Single score or grade	Evaluation on multiple competencies possible
Individual assessment	Individual or group assessment

Teachers often use constructed-response questions in classroom assessments. Figure 1.4 presents a list of tasks commonly used for performance assessments. Chapters 3 through 7 also present specific lists of tasks for each type of skill being tested.

FIGURE 1.4 COMMONLY USED PERFORMANCE ASSESSMENT TASKS

Write a letter, a newspaper article, a short story, a poem, etc.

Participate in a debate or discussion.

Draw a picture illustrating a story or article.

Explain the picture you have drawn.

List several courses of action, with the advantages and disadvantages of each.

Critique your own or someone else's work, giving examples and details.

Act in a play or skit.

Compose and/or perform a musical piece.

Choreograph and/or perform a dance.

Create a work of art.

Build a model, diorama, exhibit.

Develop an itinerary for a trip given budget and time constraints.

Present a weather forecast.

Do a survey of class opinion, and present results.

Do an interview for a class project.

Participate in a mock job interview.

Draw a map of your neighborhood.

Write a new ending for a story.

Make a poster

Propose and justify a way to solve a problem.

Predict what will happen if _____.

Answer questions beginning, "What will happen if…" or "What would you do if…" or "How would things be different if…."

Compare and contrast two stories or articles, works of art, musical pieces, dances, plays.

Critique a performance or a work of art.

Play a sport.

Make a game.

Tell a story in your own words.

Keep a journal.

Given a budget, decide what to serve at a class party.

Read a book and give a written or oral report on it.

Propose and describe an invention.

Construct a timeline.

Write a travel or tourist brochure.

Participate in a mock trial.

The more common general categories of performance assessments are:

♦ *Open-ended or extended response exercises,* or questions that require students to explore a topic orally or in writing.

Students might be asked to describe their observations made during a brief walk down the hall or outdoors, or present arguments for or against a stated opinion, or analyze a character in a passage they had read. Most other countries routinely ask students to respond orally and in writing on major tests, as well as insisting on quality day-to-day assessment (Wiggins, 1990). Essays assess a student's understanding of a subject through a written description, analysis, explanation, or summary. Essays can demonstrate how well a student uses facts in context and structures a coherent discussion. Answering essay questions effectively requires critical thinking, analysis, and synthesis. Essays and other writing samples may also be used to assess students' composition skills, including spelling, grammar, syntax, and sentence and paragraph structure.

♦ *Projects* are assignments that require sustained attention and are carried out over several hours or longer, generally (but not always) outside of regular class time.

Projects demonstrate skills and/or knowledge, are often interdisciplinary in focus, and require student initiative and creativity. Most projects require students, individually or in groups, to exhibit a visual product or perform live in class or before other audiences. Projects may be short activities such as writing and revising a poem, making a labeled collage, researching and preparing an oral or visual presentation either individually or as part of a group.

Group projects require students to work together on a complex problem that requires planning, research, internal discussion, and group presentation. This technique is particularly attractive because it facilitates cooperation and reinforces a valued outcome. The California State Department of Education reports success in using group projects.

♦ *Portfolios* are selected collections of a variety of performance-based work.

A portfolio usually includes a student's "best pieces" and the student's evaluation of their strengths and weaknesses, or perhaps some "works in progress" that illustrate the progress the student has made, as well as his understanding of what he has learned.

♦ *Behavioral assessments* cover the aspect of student performance that does not result in a tangible object.

There are two types: structured behavior, which involves a pre-established type of performance such as a skit, debate, or dance; and spontaneous behavior, which involves unplanned events such as interaction in group settings or participation in a discussion.

WHAT IS AN AUTHENTIC ASSESSMENT?

Performance assessment is an umbrella term that embraces both alternative assessment and authentic assessment. The term alternative assessment was coined to distinguish it from what it was not: traditional paper-and-pencil testing. There are two basic types of alternative assessment: one that is meaningful in an academic context, and another that has meaning and value in the context of the real world. This second type is called "authentic."

Here are the criteria for authentic assessment:

♦ A variety of assessing techniques are used;

♦ Students are given some choices on the assignment;

♦ A variety of learning modalities (i.e. auditory, visual, kinesthetic) are assessed;

♦ Students engage in problem-solving, decision-making and higher-order thinking skills;

♦ Objectives for the assessment are listed;

♦ Specific criteria for the assessment are given to students (i.e., length, format, resources to use, and due dates), called a *product descriptor;*

♦ The assessment, if long, is divided into smaller parts, with separate descriptions and due dates for each;

♦ Specific criteria for evaluating the assessment are given to students before beginning the project, with examples of what to do or not to do, called a *rubric;*

♦ Students are encouraged to plan how they will approach the task, monitor their progress, and evaluate their thinking (reflection and metacognition used);

♦ Feedback is prompt, positive in nature, and specific; and

♦ Students have a chance to share their work with others (work may be displayed).

It is easy to see how a "performance assessment" can also be authentic. Chapter 2 elaborates on how to select and write a product descriptor and a rubric for a selected assessment.

2

CHOOSING AND WRITING A PERFORMANCE ASSESSMENT AND ITS RUBRIC

With performance-based learning, the target is always a performance of some kind. Unique assessments are needed to allow teachers to judge the quality of student behavior ranging from simple responses to work completed over a long period of time. Performance assessments have two parts: a clearly defined task (called a *product descriptor*) and a list of explicit criteria for assessing student performance or product (called a *rubric*). However, these positive features of performance assessment come at a price. Performance assessment requires a greater expense of time, planning, and thought from students and teachers.

Performance assessments are typically curriculum-driven. Therefore, the first step is to decide what behavior you would like to see your students perform. Look at your text, your unit objectives, your foreign language department curriculum, a test you are getting your students ready for (i.e., AP or Regents) or even the new national standards, and decide what skill(s) you would like to check for mastery. Then choose a type of performance assessment.

Assessments are either:

- *Product related*, for example, a poster;

- *Content specific*, for example, a research project on a city or region; or

- *Task specific*, for example, writing an autobiographical incident essay, paying special attention to the verb tenses used.

After choosing the assessment (see Figure 1.4, p. 13, or any of the lists in Chapters 3, 4, 5, or 6), ask yourself the following questions, which are adapted from Herman, Aschbacher, and Winters (1992):

- Can this assessment be used to measure several outcomes at once?

  If possible, design assessments to measure several aspects of student behavior, or more than one skill. Then fewer assessments are needed.

- Does the assessment/task match the outcome(s) I'm trying to measure?

  The task shouldn't require knowledge and skills that are not related to the focus. For example, if you are trying to measure speaking skills, asking the students to read and orally summarize a difficult article penalizes students who are poor readers or who lack the background knowledge necessary to understand the article. You would, in this case, be measuring reading as much as you are measuring speaking (or perhaps even more).

- Does the assessment require the students to use critical thinking skills?

  Critical thinking skills are those that ask students to analyze, draw inferences or conclusions, critically evaluate, synthesize, create or compare. The product of the assessment should not be one in which the students have received specific instruction, because only rote memory would be tested. For example, if an essay analyzing a specific author's point of view is the assessment task, and if the class has read several articles analyzing the author's point of view and discussed these articles, then what students will produce will be a report on the content of the articles or of the class discussion, rather than the student's own analysis. A better assessment is to ask students to analyze some editorials about that author that haven't been discussed in class; they could compare and contrast the new editorial with those discussed previously, evaluate this, and draw their own conclusions, all higher-level thinking skills.

- What is the purpose of the assessment?

  The purpose of the assessment is a major factor in deciding whether to choose a short assessment (covers only a small part of curriculum and takes less than half an hour) or a long assessment.

Figure 2.1 Using *Purpose* to Select a Form of Assessment

Short	*Long*
Daily or frequent use	Culmination, i.e. final or unit test
Assessment use only	Instruction as well as assessment
Demonstration of only one concept or skill	Creativity, research, and reflection needed
Usually use more in-class time	Generally done outside class time
One single activity	Broken down into subactivities
Easier to prepare and use	More explanation, more criteria to evaluate

Longer tasks involve instruction as well as assessment—generally, research and learning of new content, or reorganizing previously learned materials into a new, individualized and/or creative format. It is better to begin using short performance assessments, due to time constraints in devising and refining, as well as in evaluating, longer assessments.

♦ Is the assessment a worthwhile use of instructional time?

Performance assessments may be time-consuming, especially individual oral assessments. Make sure that the task will be educational for the student. For instance, immediate positive feedback would let the student know where the student's strengths are, making the test an extension of the learning process.

♦ Does the assessment use engaging tasks from the "real world"?

The task should be as interesting as possible to ensure that students are willing to try their best. Is the assessment something important that students will need to do in school, or in the future? Tasks that have some connection to life outside the classroom are highly motivating.

♦ Are the tasks fair and free from bias?

Are students of different genders, cultures, and socioeconomic groups represented in your school population? Will all these students have equivalent resources, at home or at school, with which to complete the task? For example, if you are assigning a task that requires use of the Internet, make sure that all students have easy access to a computer connected to the Internet. If you require a typed paper, see that students have sufficient time to complete word processing, and so on. Don't require students to prepare a recipe that requires expensive ingredients (they may not have the money to purchase these, and won't want to admit this).

♦ Will colleagues, students and parents view this activity as being a meaningful and/or appropriate one?

If students doing this task will be subject to scorn, ridicule, or apathy on the part of others, don't assign it.

♦ Is the assessment feasible?

Will everyone have enough time, space, materials, and other resources to complete this? Does the task require knowledge and skills that you will be able to teach?

CREATING A PRODUCT DESCRIPTOR

After you have selected an assessment, and answered the above questions satisfactorily, you are ready to begin writing a *product descriptor.* This document should include:

♦ What outcome(s) will be measured;

♦ Clear instructions that are discussed and then given to students (the main portion of the product descriptor);

♦ Conditions under which the students will take the assessment, including where and when it will take place, how much time and teacher assistance they may expect, and any equipment or resource materials that may be used;

♦ Whether the student has any choices in how to respond (e.g., oral report, written report); and

♦ What scoring criteria will be used (a *rubric).*

If possible, involve someone else in your creative process, especially if you're not sure of the answers to the questions. Many schools have peer review committees to do just that—teachers present projects that they are thinking of doing, projects that they just did and really liked, or projects that they did and weren't entirely pleased with, to other teachers not necessarily in their subject area. The colleagues ask questions, and gently critique and advise each other.

On your own, with a colleague, or with students, brainstorm the characteristics students should exhibit when performing the assessment, and then categorize the characteristics. List those criteria.

This is your product descriptor. Then ask yourself several more questions:

♦ Is the task clearly defined?

Are instructions for teachers and students clear? Does the student know exactly what is expected?

♦ Are all terms defined and developmentally appropriate?

For example, if the assessment is to write an essay, do students know exactly what that means? Does an essay require a certain number of paragraphs, or a title? Make sure the product descriptor defines all terms used. Also, make sure students have the required skills to complete it: If you require an outline, have they ever done one before? If not, you may find yourself devoting a lot more time than you had planned, explaining skills that they have not yet been taught and that they may not be capable of fulfilling.

♦ Is the assessment broken down into small, manageable subdivisions?

An assessment longer than 15 minutes can usually be broken down into several portions. Give each portion its own deadline. For instance, if you are having partners do a paired activity, give them three minutes to plan their strategy, another ten minutes for the discussion, and then five minutes more to fill out an evaluation, to present their conclusions orally, or to do a peer evaluation of another group's performance.

Breaking assessments down into smaller portions serves two purposes. First, students will feel the time constraints and begin to work quickly. Second, several mini-activities seem easier to handle than one large activity with several aspects to it. This is an especially effective practice to use with mainstream students, yet any beginner will feel more comfortable taking "baby steps" in a foreign language.

Use Your Students as a Resource When Presenting the Assessment to Them

The best way to make sure that the students have the instruction correct is *not*, as many teachers seem to believe, to put it all down on a handout and read it to the students, explaining in more detail as you read. Not only is this geared specifically to audiovisual learners, many students totally tune out this typical teacher behavior. Here's a method that keeps students actively involved and make them feel some ownership for the assessment: "consult" them. This is especially easy if you are using a project or task that you have previously used.

For instance, I do a unit on famous French-speaking people: artists, writers, composers, scientists, historical figures, and so on. Each student is assigned to do a brief report with some sort of visual aid. I first ask students to imagine that they are meeting a new person. What sort of information would they like to know about that person? We list that on the board. Then I tell them this person is famous; do they have any more questions? We list the additional information on the board. This becomes part of the product descriptor; an A report will contain all that information. I then pull out three or four visual aids that past students have made (making sure that these are anonymous). Two are products that previously received A's, and two are not. I ask students to decide which of the four is the "best," and then we list why that one is the best. They usually mention things such as lots of color, readable from across the room, or has a picture.. This list becomes the rubric for an A visual aid.

If they forget a characteristic that I thought of during my brainstorming, I suggest it quietly; somehow, it becomes their suggestion if they agree with or amend it. After we have a complete list, I type it all up, and distribute it to students the next day. Not only do students feel ownership for the project, but they remember all the details that they need, have a clear picture of what they need as they begin research immediately after our discussion, and have few questions about how to do the assignment. Even better, their products are generally of much higher quality, and I no longer have parents telling me that Junior didn't know I wanted a such-and-such included in the report.

Include Scaffolding in Your Performance Assessment

The positive features of performance assessment come at a price. Performance assessment requires a greater expense of time, planning, and thought from students and teachers. One teacher reports, "We can't just march through the curriculum anymore. It's hard. I spend more time planning and more time coaching. At first, my students just wanted to be told what to do. I had to help them to start thinking."

The most profitable method to help beginning level students start thinking is to provide them with scaffolding to guide them in their efforts. Though the use of scaffolding is not very "authentic," it provides the necessary structure for them to organize their performance and better visualize the sort of effort the assessment requires. This is equally true for upper-level students who haven't taken classes from you previously, which means that this is the first such assessment that they are doing with you as their instructor.

Scaffolding can be as simple as blank lines on which they can write their answers, a map that they can fill in, or a list of references that they can use. Scaffolding can also include underlining key words in the instructions to the student or providing pictures, diagrams, or a story map (see Figure 2.4 (With Scaffolding section), p. 26, for an example) to better illustrate what should be included in the student's response. Providing some background information or context, reminding students of similar activities done previously such as classroom readings or discussions, giving hints, and/or providing students with a structured schedule or a final checklist to make sure all items are included are also forms of scaffolding. Scaffolding becomes part of the task and should be provided to all students. Figures 2.2 (p. 24), 2.3 (p. 25), and 2.4 (p. 26) are examples of performance assessment tasks both with and without scaffolding.

Reexamine any projects or assignments that you have used and check for ways to provide scaffolding (or to improve the scaffolding you already provide). For upper-level classes, scaffolding is usually used only for the first assignment and then downgraded to tips or hints/suggestions as to the possible approach to use, and scaffolding should be completely phased out by the end of the second year in order to make assessments more "authentic," and therefore more engaging.

DECIDING ON A RUBRIC

A rubric is the most commonly used method for scoring, evaluating, and grading a performance assessment. It is simply a list of the specific standards to which students will be held accountable. The rubric should be given to the students as soon as the assessment is introduced, in order to provide them with specific guidelines for completing the task, as well as a sense of how it will be graded or scored. Students using a rubric should be confident that the rubric will ensure that grading will not be done arbitrarily.

(Text continues on page 27.)

FIGURE 2.2 EXAMPLES OF PERFORMANCE
ASSESSMENT TASKS: Task 1

Without Scaffolding

List three things that you know about [foreign country].

With Scaffolding

Think about the chapter reading on [foreign country] on page 12. Open your book and look at the pictures again. Close your book and remember the video we watched last Friday. List three items that you didn't know about [country] before reading the chapter or viewing the video, or list the three most interesting things about [country] that you know. You do not need to use complete sentences, but write in [language].

1. _____

2. _____

3. _____

Now, check your work:

♦ Did you use information from the chapter?

♦ Did you write in [foreign language]?

♦ Did your partner read your list and initial it?

FIGURE 2.3 EXAMPLES OF PERFORMANCE ASSESSMENT TASKS: TASK 2

Without Scaffolding

Write a short poem in [foreign language] about someone you know.

With Scaffolding

Write a cinquain poem in [foreign language] about your best friend, a family member, or any other person you admire.

Line 1: (person's name)   _____

Line 2: (2 adjectives that describe   _____,
that person)
                                                _____

Line 3: (2 verbs, typical actions   _____,
for that person)
                                                _____

Line 4: (an adverb—how/when/   _____
why)

Line 5: (a noun that redescribes   _____
the person, may be profession,
synonym, relationship to you)

EXAMPLE: *[Name]*
                Pleasant, smiling
                Thinks, writes the poem
                Carefully
                Good grade!

Check list to do before handing in your poem:

♦ Check adjectives for gender agreement (if person is female, all adjectives need feminine ending).

♦ Check verbs in line 3 to make sure you used the third-person singular ending.

♦ Have a classmate read and critique your effort.

♦ Word process or print poem neatly on another paper for showing to class.

Due date: Monday

FIGURE 2.4 EXAMPLES OF PERFORMANCE ASSESSMENT TASKS: TASK 3

Without Scaffolding

You are an alien from another planet. Tell about yourself in an essay of no less than three pages in length, double-spaced, due Friday.

With Scaffolding

You are a visitor from another planet. Using vocabulary that we learned this year whenever possible, tell us about yourself, your people, and/or your home planet, in at least three pages, double-spaced.

Some areas that you may wish to write about are: your name, rank or profession, looks, family and pets, education, housing, food, transportation, religion, music and art, and your planet's name, location, geography, climate, and government, or your voyage here. You may wish to end the paper with your reason(s) for visiting us.

♦ Story map due Wednesday at the beginning of class

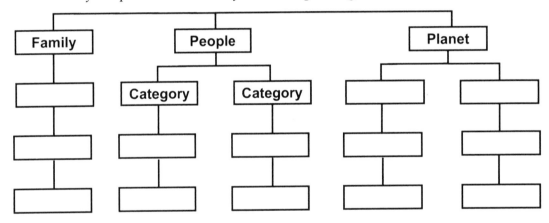

♦ Rough draft due Thursday

Checkpoints to remember:

- Take time to plan your essay on scrap paper.

- Organize your ideas carefully. Remember what you know about writing complete paragraphs.

- Check that you have used whole sentences, correct punctuation and correct spelling.

♦ Peer editing sheet Friday in class

♦ Final draft due Monday

Rubrics should be:

◆ Clear

A rubric will clearly define what is excellent, good or poor work. Students will clearly see the exact expectations and desired outcome of the assessment.

◆ Democratic

Consistent guidelines, understood by both students and the teacher, and consistently reinforced, assure students (and parents) that the teacher will not grade subjectively. Students also have a voice in determining and defining the standards.

◆ Involving

Students should always be involved in creating the rubric, as well as self- or peer assessment.

◆ Engaging

Having a rubric to look at will encourage students to evaluate their own work and strive for excellence.

TYPES OF RUBRICS

There are two types of rubrics: holistic and analytical. A holistic rubric evaluates the overall performance and rates it in a qualitative manner. Movie reviewers are holistic evaluators, giving a movie from one to four stars. The Michelin guide uses holistic ratings for hotels and restaurants. In foreign languages, the AP (Advanced Placement) exams are graded on a holistic basis. Figure 2.5 (p. 28) is an example of a holistic rubric for a writing assignment.

An analytical rubric breaks down the performance into the different levels of behavior expected, assigning each a point value (which can be weighted if desired), and which are totaled for a quantitative measure. My local newspaper food critic evaluates restaurants analytically: points are given in several separate categories such as cleanliness, atmosphere, food, and service, and then added together for an overall score. Figure 2.6 (p. 28) is an example of an analytical rubric for a written activity. A perfect score on the rubric in Figure 2.6 is 12 (4 points earned in each of three categories).

FIGURE 2.5 HOLISTIC RUBRIC FOR A WRITING ASSIGNMENT

---

1. The response does not complete the assignment. Information may be missing or inaccurate. There are problems with accuracy and logic. Overall impression: incomplete and unsatisfactory.

2. Standard barely met. Information provided is generally accurate. There may or may not be a conclusion or an opinion. If one or the other is offered, there may be problems with accuracy and logic.

3. Meets standard. Information is accurate. A logical conclusion or an opinion is offered. Writing is fluent but not interesting. The answer is lengthy rather than concise.

4. Exceeds standard. Information is accurate and writing is fluent and lively. Answer is concise and to the point. Conclusions and/or opinions are logical. Overall impression: complete and satisfactory.

FIGURE 2.6 ANALYTICAL RUBRIC FOR A WRITTEN ACTIVITY

---

	1 *Standard not met*	2 *Standard barely met*	3 *Meets standard*	4 *Exceeds standard*
Mechanics	10 or more errors: Overly simple, poorly formed sentences	Under 9 errors: Grammatically incorrect, simple sentences	Under 6 errors: Good phrasing. Mostly correct grammar	3 or fewer errors: Well-formed sentences. Proper grammar used at all times.
Word Use	Uses English and/or direct translation from dictionary. No attempt to use new vocabulary.	Uses English words. Little attempt to use new vocabulary.	Attempts to use new vocabulary. No English used.	Succeeds in using new vocabulary. No English used.
Content	Ideas are incomprehensible or inappropriate	Ideas are incomplete or copied from other sources	Ideas paraphrased from background sources, mostly complete.	Ideas completely explained and examples given. Written with ease.

While holistic rubrics are acceptable for summative work (e.g., final exams in which you must have an A, B, C, D score), analytical rubrics are more informative. Consequently, they are more developmentally helpful to students in determining strengths and weaknesses, indicating areas for improvement in future efforts and those in which progress has been made since last time, while also reinforcing the teacher's expectations.

Rubrics may be written as a checklist or a rating scale. The simplest form of rubric is the checklist. A checklist is exactly what it sounds like: a list of behaviors to look for. You record the presence or absence of that attribute by checking or circling that action. Figure 2.7 is an example of a checklist to use in evaluating an oral presentation.

FIGURE 2.7 CHECKLIST TO EVALUATE AN ORAL PRESENTATION

Spoke loud enough	Yes	No
Made eye contact	Yes	No
Used notes	Yes	No
Had a thesis	Yes	No
Used supporting examples	Yes	No
Length of presentation:	_____ minutes	

A rating scale is based on a continuum from poor to exemplary. The attributes for each level are described. Figure 2.8 is an example of a rating scale for an oral presentation.

FIGURE 2.8 A RATING SCALE FOR AN ORAL PRESENTATION

1 *Poor*	2 *Adequate*	3 *Good*	4 *Expert*
Ability to perform but skill is not apparent. Incomprehensible.	Makes serious errors but performs task.	Performs task without significant errors.	Performs task with no errors and little conscious effort.

The rating scale in Figure 2.8 has some serious flaws, but is given as a simple example of a rating scale used by many teachers. One flaw is that "serious" and "significant" are not clearly defined. Also, many people might prefer to have the scale begin at zero, as a student with no evident ability should perhaps receive no points whatsoever, but I like to give at least one point for attempting the activity rather than refusing outright to do it.

The rating scale is obviously much more specific and informative, but also a bit more difficult to use, because the behaviors are not as "black and white" as those of the checklist. When using a rating scale, try to use an even number of points (four-point scales such as in Figure 2.8 are the most common) because then there is no middle. Many people are tempted, if the product or behavior is not clearly outstanding, to assign a score in the middle of a range. This is called *central tendency.* If there is no middle score, they must then make a decision whether the product falls to the better-quality or lower-quality side of the center.

WHAT MAKES A GOOD RUBRIC?

Now that you have decided whether to use holistic or analytical rubric, a checklist or a rating scale, and have a list of behaviors supplied by students during the brainstorming you did with them, it is time to write the rubric. A well-written rubric that will be easy to use has the following:

- ♦ The standard (best possible performance, "excellent") should be written first. This is the level that you want all students to achieve, and it should be challenging.

- ♦ Use demonstrative verbs.

- ♦ Keep to observable behaviors. Avoid negatives (i.e., write "Begins without preparation" rather than "Does not prepare"). Define all terms. Students must be able to easily interpret or understand the rubric (e.g., define "original" or "creative"). Be specific; for example, instead of "many errors" use "six or more errors." When possible, avoid relying on adverbs and adjectives to define distinctions between levels of performance. Try to identify clear distinctions in behaviors.

- ♦ Make sure the behaviors are directly aligned with instruction. Don't ask students to exhibit skills that they were not previously taught or shown. The behaviors listed should be those found in curriculum.

♦ Assess process as well as product: how they behave during research or prewriting should be included in the rubric, not just the final product.

♦ Allow for the assessment task to be critiqued and revised.

♦ Check the number of points given. One to four points (holistic) is adequate only for a summative activity. Formative tasks may wish to include more points in the scale, with more than one level of "unacceptable" to see how close to the "passing" cut-off student performance is.

♦ Generic rubrics are more useful. Creating rubrics is time-consuming and the more often they can be applied, the better. It is also more informative for students if the same rubric is used again and again, as they can see themselves making progress when they get a higher score on the second assessment than on the first.

When the rubric is written, reread it with the following adjustments in mind:

♦ Where will the line between "acceptable" and "unacceptable" be? Between 1 and 2, or between 2 and 3? Higher standards may be used for an easier assessment or a more capable class.

♦ Is the distance between points/levels similar? The difference between a 2 and a 3 performance should not be more than the difference between a 3 and a 4 performance.

♦ Are there too many criteria? In trying to be thorough, an unwieldy assessment instrument may be constructed, with so many behaviors being evaluated that the rubric is time-consuming to fill out and/or behaviors will need to be taped (audio or video) in order to repeat them several times for the purposes of assessment.

♦ Are all criteria equally important? Weighting one area may be something you should consider. Is the content or the appearance of a paper more important, or are they of equal importance? How serious are errors such as accent marks when compared to sentence length? Weighting is especially important when using a holistic scale.

DON'T FORGET THE STUDENTS

As I wrote earlier in this chapter, after beginning with a rough idea of what criteria you would like to see, ask students to contribute to both the criteria ("product descriptor") and the rubric. For example, ask them what makes a TV program good, list those attributes, and then help them organize them into a rubric for their own video presentation. Then have them discriminate between A and B level work. They may have good ideas to add to the criteria that you had already thought important, but be careful never to relinquish control of the project entirely to the students.

PILOTING THE RUBRIC

After the rubric is typed, distribute it to the students and have them rate a few possible or probable efforts (either using past student work not previously seen, teacher-constructed examples, or "what if" discussion). If they do not score the work as you would have, make any revisions necessary to the rubric. Keeping samples of student work from year to year, especially the exemplary work, is a very good idea. If students see quality work before beginning the assignment, then the general standard gets better from year to year. I find that my "exemplary" for the first year I give an assessment often gets downgraded to a "good" as students grasp expectations and strive for excellence at a higher level than the examples presented.

Use your first draft over a period of time as you observe students in the classroom. Continue to review your rubrics until you believe they provide a comprehensive picture of levels of attainment of proficiency.

SUMMARY

There are many advantages to using performance assessments with good product descriptors and rubrics. These advantages include:

♦ Students know all the desired attributes of the performance.

♦ An assignment no longer involves guesswork about what is desirable (no "gotcha" from the teacher). Excellence is defined by students and teacher working together, and is therefore both expected and understood.

♦ Students feel capable of achieving a higher quality of work. All teachers using quality rubrics report that student work improves dramatically.

The Chapters 3 through 6 will take us from the primarily theoretical content of Chapters 1 and 2 to actual practice of the four competencies of foreign languages, with actual examples of assessments and rubrics from instructors all over the United States, in a variety of languages.

3

FROM THEORY TO PRACTICE: ORAL ASSESSMENTS

The following list is a fairly complete summary of activities ordinarily used for oral performance assessments:

anecdote	dramatization	monologue
ballad/rap/song	explanation	narration
book report	fairy tale	newscast
campaign speech	free verse	oath
choral reading/speech	interview	recipe
debate	jingle/ad campaign	riddle
demonstration	joke	role-play
dialogue	lecture	seminar
discussion	lesson	skit
documentary	mock interview	weather report

As audio and video become increasingly available to record performances, the use of oral presentations for assessment is likely to increase. Oral presentations enable students to verbalize knowledge, and are essential to foreign language teaching; fluency can be assessed only by listening to students speak. As we all know, unless oral testing is part of the curriculum, students may never see communication skills as a desirable goal.

The best feature of oral assessments is the speed at which they can be completed and graded/scored. Oral performances may be evaluated using either holistic or analytical rubrics, which will probably be very similar to those rubrics that are used for assessing writing tasks. These rubrics may assign points or percentages for each aspect. Here are some initial suggestions:

+ Keep the number of criteria down to a manageable number.

+ Keep the criteria straightforward and clear to you and to the students.

+ Keep in mind that assessments should be meaningful and cover only important content.

+ Develop an easy method of scoring.

HOLISTIC SCORING

Here is an example of a four-point holistic system for oral assessment:

Level 1:   Made an effort, but really didn't understand the question.

Level 2:   Some understanding, but limited.

Level 3:   Good understanding, but answer not thorough.

Level 4:   Good understanding, quality answer.

The SUE method is an example of a three-point, part-holistic, part-analytical scoring system that is suitable for short oral assessments. I am including it under the holistic aspect because it would be scored using a plus sign, a check mark, a minus sign, and a zero system:

SUE Method

Success: Did the student successfully accomplish what was assigned?

Understanding: How easy was the response to understand?

Effort: Was the speaker making an effort to communicate rather than just answer briefly?

	S	U	E	Grade
Student 1	+	+	✔	B
Student 2	+	✔	✔	B–/C+
Student 3	✔	✔	✔	C
Student 4	+	+	+	A
Student 5	✔	–	0	D

ANALYTICAL RUBRICS

Many foreign language departments have developed oral proficiency guidelines. An Internet search using the words "oral proficiency" will turn up many examples, or you can check the archives on FL-TEACH (see the Bibliography for the address). All of the oral proficiency guidelines that I have seen are analytical rubrics. Figure 3.1 shows the simplest form of an analytical rubric.

FIGURE 3.1 THE SIMPLEST FORM

---

10 pt. for accuracy (grammar/vocabulary)

10 pt. for fluency (pronunciation/flow)

10 pt. for overall (quantity, variety of vocabulary + forms)

TOTAL: 30 points

What makes Figure 3.1 analytical is that, instead of grading the overall performance, it is divided into several aspects, each of which is evaluated individually. The above rubric does have some serious flaws. First, it is not defined clearly enough for students. Does each grammar/vocabulary error take one point off—for example, "2 errors = 8 pt."—or will this be applied holistically by the teacher, as in, "I think this is better than average, but not perfect so I'll write down an 8"?

Second, it is not clear what an acceptable score is for this activity. Obviously, everyone should strive for all 30 points, but what is a passing or failing effort? Figure 3.2 (p.38) is a slightly better analytical rubric.

The rubric in Figure 3.2 is better than the simple rubric of Figure 3.1 as it clearly shows what grades will be received, but it is still not entirely clear. Does *any* characteristic described in the D range earn a D for the performance? For example, if the student speaks smoothly, using a variety of structures, but uses an English word repeatedly, is it a D? This sort of confusion would normally be cleared up through use of examples (it might be a good idea to have the students evaluate a couple of sample speeches on tape using the above rubric, so that they could see how it might be applied) and class discussion, or additional clarification of terms such as "minimal errors" by the teacher. Figure 3.3 (p. 39) is what a clearer and more usable rubric might look like.

(Text continues on page 40.)

FIGURE 3.2 A SLIGHTLY BETTER RUBRIC

Oral Proficiency Guidelines

♦ An A student:

- Makes minimal errors,
- Uses rich and varied vocabulary,
- Speaks with excellent pronunciation,
- Speaks smoothly without stopping, and
- Uses a variety of sentence structures.

♦ A B student:

- Demonstrates competence, but makes some errors,
- Makes only minor errors that do not interfere seriously with communication,
- Uses a broad range of vocabulary, and
- Has good pronunciation.

♦ A C student:

- Demonstrates competence, but makes frequent errors,
- Probably would not be entirely understood by a native speaker,
- Speaks with mediocre pronunciation, and
- Hesitates when speaking, but shows an awareness of correct usage by self-correcting.

♦ A D student:

- Makes so many errors that the student cannot be understood,
- Hesitates often,
- Pronounces the language poorly,
- Uses English occasionally, and
- Has major weaknesses in grammar and pronunciation.

♦ An F student:

- Makes no attempt to speak or is completely incomprehensible,
- Has weak vocabulary and/or uses primarily English to respond, and
- Did not respond appropriately for the task assigned.

FIGURE 3.3 A CLEARER AND MORE USABLE RUBRIC

Level 1 Speaking Tasks—Analytic Rubric

- Task Completion
  1—Minimal attempt to complete the task and/or responses frequently inappropriate,
  2—Partial completion of the task, responses mostly appropriate yet undeveloped,
  3—Completion of the task, responses appropriately and adequately developed, and
  4—Superior completion of the task, responds with elaboration.

- Comprehensibility
  1—Responses barely comprehensible,
  2—Responses mostly comprehensible, requiring interpretation by the listener,
  3—Responses comprehensible, requiring minimal interpretation, and
  4—Responses readily comprehensible.

- Fluency
  1—Speech halting and uneven with long pauses and/or incomplete thoughts,
  2—Speech slow and/or with frequent pauses, few or no incomplete thoughts,
  3—Some hesitation but manages to continue and complete thoughts, and
  4—Speech continuous with little stumbling.

- Pronunciation
  1—Frequent errors, little or no communication,
  2—Occasional problems with communication,
  3—No interference with communication, and
  4—Communication with ease.

- Vocabulary
  1—Inadequate and/or inaccurate use of vocabulary,
  2—Somewhat inadequate and/or inaccurate use of vocabulary,
  3—Adequate and accurate use of vocabulary, and
  4—Rich use of vocabulary with frequent attempts at elaboration.

What makes the rubric in Figure 3.3 better than the two previously given is that it clearly shows what areas will be evaluated and what the desired behaviors for each area are. The above divisions are, of course, not the only ones. Decide what behaviors are most important to you, or those that will insure success on the examination students are practicing for. Some other headings that might be used are:

- Grammar accuracy;
- Complexity of grammatical structures used;
- Quantity of response (especially for a performance that must exceed a certain time limit);
- Completeness of response;
- Variety of responses (grammar or vocabulary);
- Strategic competency;
- Sociolinguistic competency; and
- Discourse competency.

TEACHING STUDENTS TO BE BETTER ORAL PERFORMERS

The last three headings on the list above are drawn from Linda Paulus' article (1998), which was based on Krashen and Terrell's theories on language acquisition, in which Paulus discusses teaching students those concepts in order to evaluate them and help them evaluate their own progress as well. Strategic competency is basically the speaker's command of "coping" strategies—phrases such as "Again, please!," "I don't understand," and "What does X mean?"—plus circumlocution techniques. Sociolinguistic competency is the students' ability to speak in a culturally appropriate manner; examples include the correct usage of *tu/Usted*, *tu/vous*, or *du/Sie*, as well as traditional greeting and leave-taking procedures. Discourse competency is a command of enough vocabulary to be easily understandable and be able to use less strategic competency to communicate.

CONVERTING POINTS TO LETTER GRADES

Most analytical rubrics use a point-based scoring system. If this is done, students need to be told what score would be the lowest "acceptable" score. Figure 3.4 is an interesting formula from Fairfax County Public Schools in Virginia that I found on the Internet at www.fcps.k12.va.us/DIS/OHSICS/forlang/PALS/

index.htm. It is used to convert a point-based analytical assessment to a "gradebook score."

FIGURE 3.4 CONVERSION FORMULA

♦ Step 1: Determine the Raw Score

- Determine the points attained for each domain (i.e., Task Completion) Half points may be given, i.e., 0.5, 1.5, 2.5, or 3.5. Add up the points from all the domains to get the Raw Score.

♦ Step 2: Convert the Raw Score to a Percentage Score

- Using the chart below, determine the Converted Percentage Score. If the Raw Score included a half-point, assign a percentage score in between the percents given for whole numbers. For example, a raw score of 20.5 would become a converted percentage score of 92.4 (halfway between 91.3 and 93.5).

♦ Step 3: Determine the "Gradebook Score"

- If you use percents in your gradebook (weighted or unweighted), enter in your gradebook the Converted Percentage Score as determined above in Step 2.

- If you use points in your gradebook, use the Conversion Chart or the following formula:

    Converted Percentage Score × maximum points/100 = student's point score.

TYPES OF ORAL ASSESSMENTS

INTERVIEWS

Particularly with younger children or lower levels, interviews are the form of assessment likely to elicit longer and more informative responses. The most common type is the interview in which a question is asked and students answer it in the foreign language; for example, *Como se llama? Comment t'appelles-tu? Wie heißt du?* Another variation that tests grammar along with fluency is to provide a sentence in English for the student to translate into the target language, such as "What is your name?" An even more creative way might be to hold an interview-style conversation (or a simulated telephone conversation) involving vocabulary from a unit; for example, asking a student what they would like to eat and drink for dinner that night.

Because interviews involve less complex answers, the grading rubric could lbe as simple as the rubric in Figure 3.5.

FIGURE 3.5 A SIMPLE RUBRIC FOR INTERVIEWS

0—No reply/didn't answer question at all

1—One word answer

2—Sentence answer with obvious major error(s)

3—Sentence answer, but minimal or no errors.

Figure 3.6 is another two-step version that will yield a score that easily converts to a percentage, as it has 10 points possible.

FIGURE 3.6 A TWO-STEP RUBRIC

◆ Ease

　3　Answered question once after hearing it at normal speed

　2　Answered question only after it was repeated

　1　Answered question only after it was repeated very slowly and/or reworded

　0　Made no attempt to answer

◆ Fluency

　7　Extensive response, easily comprehended

　6　Appropriate shorter response, easily comprehended

　5　Appropriate response, but only comprehensible by someone used to foreigners

　4　Partially appropriate response, but very difficult to understand

　2　Inappropriate response

　0　No response

GRADING GROUP ORAL BEHAVIOR IN CLASS

If you want a weekly participation grade, then start with a clean seating chart each week. During group or partner work, using codes, mark down what you hear. The codes could be something like this (FL = the target foreign language):

5   quality FL, no English, speaks with ease

4   good FL, no English, speaks with some ease

3   no English, speaks haltingly but tries

2   mostly in FL, a few English words

1   trying to speak FL but has too much English interference

0   nonsense FL or no FL

When students are speaking, either walk around the room or sit in the center of the room and listen. When you hear them speak, write down the code next to their name. You don't need to worry about writing down the same amount of codes (i.e., five codes) for every person. At the end of the week, look at the codes, throw out the highest and lowest for each student, and average the others together. That gives you a number between 0 and 5, which you relate to a letter scale or percentage scale.

APPEALING TO MULTIPLE LEARNING STYLES

An oral assessment, like any foreign language performance, is best suited to students whose main learning style is Linguistic, but these may be adapted to help students with other learning styles in the following ways:

◆ Incorporate the use of gestures or props to assist primarily Bodily-Kinesthetic learners.

◆ Use a graphic organizer such as a Venn diagram for Logical-Mathematical or Spatial learners. (For example, before asking students to discuss how a holiday is celebrated, have them complete a graphic organizer that lists the celebrations in order, or compare/contrast them with ours.)

◆ Provide a cue such as a picture, poster, chart, diagram or map to provide cues for Spatial learners who are primarily visual. (Example: Bring in the picture of a famous person and introduce them to the class. Tell name, age, profession, what they look like, and something that you and this person have in common).

- Have students sing or recite a nursery rhyme or poem with rhythm and rhyme to appeal to those with Musical intelligence.

- Have oral assessments such as skits with partners to involve Interpersonal learners.

EXAMPLES OF ORAL ASSESSMENTS

The rest of this chapter consists of oral assessments contributed by colleagues; all of them classroom teachers, along with samples of performances, their grading methods, hints, and comments.

TELLING STORIES (TPRS)

This oral performance assessment comes from Lynette Lang at Hampshire High School in Hampshire, IL:

> I run a TPRS class, and for oral assessments, I use a chain story. Once the vocabulary and associated grammar and story line of the unit have been internalized, I give an oral prompt to start the story with a twist. The new story takes on a life of its own as each student adds his or her piece of the plot. This is usually very amusing and quick (10 minutes).

> I give an A for the following categories: audible, logical, correct, and sufficient content; B for an above average attempt in all areas, with some mistakes and stutters; C if the student can at least re-tell where we are in the plot. This lets me know that they are paying attention and are able to understand and retell in their own words but are not fluent enough to deviate from the paved path. If the student can't say anything, they get a 0. Most everyone can produce A/B dialogue.

> I do many of these, which count for a quiz grade. The best part of this activity is that the students really get creative and I see what I term fluency."

CONVERSATIONS

This oral performance assessment comes from Mary Young, Norte Vista High School, Riverside, CA:

> I just gave oral quizzes a couple of days ago as part of the final. Here's what I did.

> My text features language functions along with vocabulary and grammar. There are sets of expressions to use in certain situations

(e.g., giving an opinion on films, inviting someone to do something, accepting/refusing an invitation…). I had the students copy these onto a single sheet over time, and we did mini-skits (i.e., pairs, A/B circles, cocktail party) using brief scenarios from these function lists. I gave them the outline of what to talk about, modeled a dialog (using puppets), and turned them loose. I spiraled the mini-skits, adding a new feature each time until they had a decent skit using their expressions. That is the way we practiced.

For the test itself, I called up two kids at random, gave each of them a card outlining the kind of thing they were supposed to cover, gave them a general scenario, and a two- or three-minute time limit. I had the topics listed across the top of the page, their names down the side, and marked a plus if they handled the topic well, a check if it was just OK, and a minus if it was inadequate (i.e., unintelligible, non-existent, or showed they hadn't understood their partner's question). Because they were working in "unequal" pairs, I encouraged them to expand their questions if their partner didn't seem to have an answer. So, when Trong asked Cheri, *Qu'est-ce que tu veux manger?* and she didn't answer for a few seconds, he rephrased the question to *Qu'est-ce que tu prends comme sandwich?* (Still no answer, so he prompts: *Tu veux un sandwich au fromage? Au jambon? Au thon?*) He's showing his control of the language, even though his partner isn't giving him anything to play with. She caught on at this point and was able to respond appropriately. To get the grade on this I looked for the overall number of +s holistically.

TELLING STORIES (VIDEOTAPED)

Here is a new idea for oral assessment that frees the teacher during class time. It was provided by Susan Gross from Colorado Springs, Colorado.

I use a camcorder and an assistant so that I can continue interacting with my class. I make up two different illustrations of stories, about eight frames in length, cutting and pasting pictures to make the stories.

The camcorder is set up on a tripod in the back corner of the classroom with a blackboard on wheels back there to separate the "recording studio" from the rest of the class. The assistant is back there to run things. The assistant is usually a student's parent, but you could use the office aide, library aide, your own student aide, or even a volunteer from class. Essentially all they do is push the pause button.

Each "testee" is allowed to look at his story for up to two minutes before beginning to talk. The second student gets story #2 and is looking at it while the first student talks. When the first student finishes, he sets down story #1, goes to get the third student who picks up story #1 and looks at it while the second student is talking, and so forth.

I do half the class one day and half the class the next day, with very little disruption of my classroom. I use a different tape for each period, so after school I grade an entire class on one tape.

Figure 3.7 is a copy of the rubric Susan uses to evaluate these performances, and which she shares with the students before the evaluation.

FIGURE 3.7 ORAL RUBRIC

Comprehensibility	Vocabulary	Correctness of language	Risk-taking, signs of improvement
5 Story was easy to understand. It was a complete story, with a beginning, middle, and end.	**5** Lots of detail. A wide variety of vocabulary words (more than just from current lesson.)	**5** Good pronunciation. Almost no grammar mistakes. Language flowed smoothly.	**5** Story was creative, told with expression. You used transition words, inserted colorful comments. You found a way to communicate entirely in French.
3 Story was fairly easy to follow, but there were a few rough spots (hesitation or groping for words.)	**3** You used the vocabulary necessary to tell the story. The basic vocabulary was used correctly.	**3** Mostly correct, but you had some difficulty with pronunciation or grammar.	**3** Some vocal expression and creativity. The story was told correctly some elaboration.
1 Story was difficult to follow. Speech was very choppy.	**1** The story lacked needed words or misused words.	**1** Little attempt made to pronounce correctly. Significant errors in usage or grammar.	**1** Monotone. You resorted to English. You only did the minimum to get by.

Contributed by Susan Gross

ORAL FRENCH EXAM: SHORT ANSWER

Figure 3.8, provided by Sandra Howard of Marin Catholic High School in Kentfield, CA, is a good example of a short, easy-to-grade oral exam with visual cues, to test activities in the passé composé tense and weather in the imparfait.

FIGURE 3.8 DISCOVERING FRENCH ROUGE UNITÉ 3 EXAMEN ORAL

Why *didn't* these people do the following things?

Contributed by Sandra Howard

ORAL EXAMS: IN PAIRS OR ALONE

This is what Kelly Ferguson of Pioneer Westfield High School in Westfield, WI, does for final exams in her classes:

> In Spanish 2 to 4, I gave students a list of about 10 questions I might ask. They signed up to take the test in pairs or alone. I let them decide if they wanted a partner or not. Each person got an individual grade, but the thought of an oral exam really scared some so they liked the moral support.
>
> To grade these, I made a rubric with five categories (pronunciation, verb forms, vocabulary, sentence structure, and overall) and rated each student 1 to 4 in each category.
>
> My Spanish 1 students did the same, but instead of questions I had them compose a dialogue. The rubric was identical (that way I could just run off copies of one sheet for each class). Because this was so wide open, I told them I'd be *much* more impressed if they incorporated the simple food vocabulary or the regular preterit we just started into the dialogue. Many students challenged themselves to actually *use* this stuff!

Yet another very good oral assessment that incorporates both a product descriptor and an analytical rubric is the one in Figure 3.9, which was provided by Vernon E. Jacobs, Associate Superintendent of Glendale Union School District, Glendale, AZ.

FIGURE 3.9 LEVEL 1 TO 2 SPEAKING PERFORMANCE ASSESSMENT

Purpose:
1. The speaking performance rubric is used to evaluate samples of oral communicative skills.
2. It can be easily applied to any sample of extended speech. The criteria of "Fluency" necessitates more than a simple one sentence response.

Design:
1. The assessment design requires that the student orally
   a. responds to a series of three (3) open-ended prompts. 20 seconds are allowed for each.
   b. describes a picture (or series of 3 pictures) for one minute.
2. The assessment can be administered "live" or recorded on tape for later evaluation.

Further enhancements:
1. When using the recorded method, the student can listen to his responses and "script" (write) them on paper. He can then analyze his sample and self-evaluate using the rubric below. Additionally, he can indicate corrections as evidence of extended knowledge.
2. The rubric provides a standard that can be used in cooperative group evaluation of others' taped samples.

	Outstanding	Highly Successful	Successful	Not Yet Successful
Communication	For the level of study, the oral response is: • predominantly comprehensible • appropriate • varied in detail	• comprehensible for the most part • appropriate • somewhat detailed	• generally comprehensible • appropriate • limited or repetitious in detail	• incomprehensible *or* • inappropriate *or* • inadequate
Accuracy of Spoken Language: includes appropriate use of: • vocabulary • pronunciation • level appropriate grammar	For the level of study, the oral response demonstrates: • strong control of language usage and is • virtually free of significant errors	• good control of language usage and may have • occasional significant errors	• adequate control of language usage and may have • some significant errors	• may have excessive errors *or* • is difficult to comprehend *or* • is inadequate
Fluency	For the level of study, the oral response demonstrates: • an obvious ease of expression • speech that predominantly flows smoothly	• an ease of expression • speech that flows smoothly most of the time	• a limited ease of expression • speech that flows smoothly only some of the time	• an awkwardness of expression *or* • speech that does not flow smoothly *or* • is inadequate

Contributed by Glendale Union School District, Glendale, AZ

ORAL PRESENTATION RUBRIC

Kate Bourque of Murdock Middle High School of Winchendon, MA, explains her oral presentation rubric, a general one used for all presentations in her class, as follows:

> I designed the rubric that I use for oral presentations in my Spanish classroom. I just took bits and pieces of rubrics and put mine together, along with the assistance of my students. The students made lists of what they expected from a good presentation and we went from there.

> This rubric is pretty basic. To receive an A on a presentation, one must complete *all* the expectations under the A, and the same follows for the rest of the rubric. I also include an evaluation form that each class member does on the presenter(s) and one the presenter(s) does on themselves or each other. The student then receives a grade on the compiled data, my input as the teacher, and the peer input.

Kate has also included a copy of an evaluation of a A presentation on Peru. Figures 3.10 through 3.15 are the different parts of the rubric. Figure 3.10 is the sample rubric. Figure 3.11 (p. 53) explains why the group received the grade it did. As the group made its presentation, Kate made notes on the rubric form, as shown in Figure 3.12 (p. 54). Figure 3.13 (p. 55) is a sample evaluation form for this presentation. The evaluation form is completed by the presenters (Figure 3.14, p. 56) and by members of the audience (Figure 3.15, p. 57).

(Text continues on page 58.)

FIGURE 3.10 SAMPLE RUBRIC

ORAL PRESENTATION RUBRIC
LA CLASE DE ESPAÑOL

A   * thesis clearly stated
- presentation was coherent and well organized
- presenter(s) speak in a clear voice
- speaker(s) makes eye contact with everyone in the audience
- speaker(s) do not have nervous habits
- presentation well organized with a beginning, middle, and end
- information is complete and accurate
- clear evidence of research
- visual aides are well done and used to make presentation more interesting and meaningful (handouts included in this)
- appropriate length
- speaker(s) show enthusiasm of topic
- speakers(s) involve the audience

B   * thesis clearly stated
- presentation was coherent and well organized (beginning, middle, and end)
- information complete and accurate
- clear evidence of research
- visual aides are well done and used to make presentation more interesting and meaningful (this includes handouts)
- appropriate length
- some eye contact
- a few nervous habits
- speaker(s) involve some of the audience

C   * thesis stated
- presentation shows little organization; rambles or may seem like a list of facts
- clear evidence of research
- eye contact with very few in the audience
- spoke too fast or too slow
- very little use and/or poor use of visuals
- not long enough
- speaker(s) exhibits some nervous habits that distract from presentation
- speaker(s) involve little to none of the audience

D
* * presenter(s) difficult to hear
* speaker(s) show little enthusiasm in topic
* not long enough
* no eye contact
* read like a report
* presentation shows little organization, unclear purpose, unclear relationship and/or transition
* lack of evidence of research
* no visual aids
* speaker(s) show nervous habits which distract from presentation
* speaker(s) do not involve the audience

F
* * no real thesis stated
* could not hear presenter(s)
* speaker(s) show no enthusiasm in topic
* no eye contact
* read from a paper, like a report
* presentation shows no organization, unclear purpose, unclear transition (no beginning, middle, or end)
* no evidence of research
* no visual aides
* not long enough
* audience not involved at all
* no details or examples
* not a well chosen topic for the audience

Courtesy of Kate Bourque

FIGURE 3.11 EXPLANATION PAGE

This group deserved the grade they received, because it was clear what their chosen topic was, they involved the audience through items shown from Peru, a knowledge of research of Peru by giving facts about Peru and pointing items out on a map of Peru. This group covered all the necessities on the rubric to receive an A letter grade.

Attached you will find their peer evaluation of the presentation, the rubric that I use with the notes on it and the group evaluation.

Courtesy of Kate Bourque

FIGURE 3.12 RUBRIC WITH NOTES

ORAL PRESENTATION RUBRIC
LA CLASE DE ESPAÑOL

A (*) thesis clearly stated *Peru*

(•) presentation was coherent and well organized

all 3 (•) presenter(s) speak in a clear voice

(•) speaker(s) makes eye contact with everyone in the audience

(•) speaker(s) do not have nervous habits

involved audience with handouts, items from Peru, photos from Peru (•) presentation well organized with a beginning, middle, and end *facts on Peru*

(•) information is complete and accurate *map of Peru*

(•) clear evidence of research *went to Peru!!* *pointed out items on map*

(•) visual aides are well done and used to make presentation more interesting and meaningful (handouts included in this)

(•) appropriate length *20 minutes, only needed 7-10 min.* *2 languages*

(•) speaker(s) show enthusiasm of topic *1. Spanish*

(•) speaker(s) involve the audience *handouts, items question period @ end.* *2. Quechua*

B * thesis clearly stated

Pacific Ocean = rock beaches dump trash into ocean • presentation was coherent and well organized (beginning, middle, and end)

• information complete and acccurate

• clear evidence of research *poster w/ info. on it about Peru*

• visual aides are well done and used to make presentation more interesting and meaningful (this includes handouts)

• appropriate length

• some eye contact *students did ask questions, seemed interested in knowing about another country*

• a few nervous habits

• speaker(s) involve some of the audience

C * Thesis stated

one week in Lima one week in Juárez • presentation shows little organization; rambles or may seem like a list of facts

• clear evidence of research

• eye contact with very few in the audience

• spoke too fast or too slow

• very little use and/or poor use of visuals

• not long enough

poncho bolsa photos money pottery journal of trip stuffed bear made from llama fur • speaker(s) exhibits some nervous habits that distract from presentation

• speaker(s) involve little to none of the audience

D * presenter(s) difficult to hear

• speaker(s) show little enthusiasm in topic

• not long enough

Courtesy of Kate Bourque

FIGURE 3.13 SAMPLE EVALUATION FORM

Nombre_____ la fecha_____

Evaluation Form

1. Presenter(s)_____
2. On a scale of 1 – 10, rate this presentation in the following
categories:

_____ interesting   _____ informative   _____ well-prepared

3. What was this presentation about?

4. List one thing that you learned from this presentation.

5. List one thing you disliked about the presentation?

Individual/Group Assessment Form

1. List what each individual did in your group: (research,
posters, speaking,...)

2. Positive experiences of the presentation:

3. Negative experiences of the presentation:

4. Comments:

5. What was the topic of your presentation?

Courtesy of Kate Bourque

FIGURE 3.14 EVALUATION FILLED OUT BY PRESENTER

Nombre_____ la fecha_____

Evaluation Form

1. Presenter(s)_____
2. On a scale of 1 – 10, rate this presentation in the following categories:

_____ interesting   _____ informative   _____ well-prepared

3. What was this presentation about?

4. List one thing that you learned from this presentation.

5. List one thing you disliked about the presentation?

Individual/Group Assessment Form

1. List what each individual did in your group: (research, posters, speaking,...)

   I did poster and lots of research and explanations of the basic facts of Peru.
   Heidi did all the stuff from Peru.
   Kristin made a poster.

2. Positive experiences of the presentation:
   we got a good grade.

3. Negative experiences of the presentation:
   Nothing.

4. Comments:
   Everybody took our presentation seriously and payed attention.

5. What was the topic of your presentation?
   Peru

Courtesy of Kate Bourque

FIGURE 3.15 EVALUATION FILLED OUT BY AUDIENCE MEMBER

Nombre_____ la fecha_____

Evaluation Form

1. Presenter(s)_____

2. On a scale of 1 – 10, rate this presentation in the following categories:

___9___ interesting   ___10___ informative   ___10___ well-prepared

3. What was this presentation about?
   Peru.

4. List one thing that you learned from this presentation.
   Everything in Peru is cheaper,

5. List one thing you disliked about the presentation?
   The video was a little too long.

Individual/Group Assessment Form

1. List what each individual did in your group: (research, posters, speaking,...)

2. Positive experiences of the presentation:

3. Negative experiences of the presentation:

4. Comments:

5. What was the topic of your presentation?

Courtesy of Kate Bourque

PHONE MESSAGE

This oral performance assessment comes from is a creative homework assignment:

> I am fortunate to have a telephone in my classroom, with voice mail. One of my favorite assignments is to require students to phone my voice mail and leave a message that will use vocabulary and grammatical structures that we are currently working on in class. Here is one example of such an assignment and the rubric used to evaluate it. I might also add that I usually play the conversations for the class on the speakerphone after I have graded their contributions and given them their scored copy of the rubric. This way the students can both verify their own performance and see how theirs compares with those of their classmates. This is a very high-interest activity!

Telephone Call

This weekend you must call my voice mail and leave a message: 665-2186 Extension 1125. Tell me the following:

- An appropriate greeting and your name;
- Two things you did this weekend;
- Someone you saw this weekend; and
- Something you would like to do this week in class.

Don't forget to use the past tense for the weekend events."

Excellent	Adequate	Unacceptable
Includes all five items on list.	Includes all 5 items on list.	Missing one item.
Speaks without hesitation.	Speaks hesitantly.	Does not pronounce clearly.
Uses correct pronunciation and grammar (may self-correct).	Makes 1 error in pronunciation/grammar.	Makes several errors.

4

FROM THEORY TO PRACTICE: WRITTEN ASSIGNMENTS

The following list is a fairly complete summary of activities ordinarily used for assessments of writing proficiency:

advertisement	editorial essay	magazine/news article	questionnaire
autobiography	fact file	metaphor	quiz
biography	fairy tale/myth	movie review	recipe
book report	glossary	newsletter	report
booklet/brochure	guidebook	new story end-ing	review
business letter	handbook	notes	riddle
cartoon	handout	oath	script
celebrity profile	headline	observation sheet	scroll
checklist	interview script	outline	short story
comic book	job description	pamphlet	slogan
commercial script	joke	parody	story problem
comparison	journal	pen pal letter	survey
computer program	law	petition	telegram
creative writing	lesson plan	play	travel log
critique	list	poem	yearbook entry
description	log	poster	
dialogue	lyrics	prediction	
diary/journal		puppet show	

The purpose of a writing assessment is to communicate a thought or idea in writing, demonstrating proficiency in the target language. Often, however, we have difficulty deciding how to grade them.

Writing assessments are actually the easiest of all to do. First, writing is the form that most tests provided by textbook companies handle best. Generally, today, every end-of-chapter test asks students for a short essay on a prompted topic (e.g., "Tell about when you were in sixth grade. What school did you go to? Where did you live? Who were your friends? What did you do with them?" or "Pretend you live in [another time, place, or culture]. Write a story that tells how you spend a typical day, including what you do, what you wear, what you eat, and where you live.").

If you don't like the tests provided by your text, see an English teacher. They regularly have students write authentic things, and some may have some unique ideas (or a couple of good writing resource books you can borrow). They are also invaluable resources for grading rubrics; I have often used or adapted an English rubric for grading organization, mechanics, style, and quality of expression. The state of Indiana, where I live, has a good holistic rubric that every teacher displays in their classroom, and with which students are quite familiar.

BRAINSTORMING

Brainstorming is a valuable introductory technique. Tell students to write, individually or with a partner, a list of words or phrases they know about a chosen topic. Give them a short amount of time so that they get right to work. Use competition to encourage output; give a prize of some sort for the most words. Find out who has the most by having one person from each group, in turn, go to the board or the overhead and write a word that hasn't been written yet. The last group able to write a new word wins. Now you have a good basis for them to begin organizing thoughts to write a rough draft.

ROUGH DRAFTS

Rough drafts are an important step in writing. Here are several suggestions on how to handle these and make them part of an assessment (thereby saving yourself a lot of grading by the time the final selection is handed in):

◆ Require a rough draft, and, using a rubric, give a grade that reflects what the grade would be if it were the final version. This is usually a good motivator for students to want to fix it up a bit more.

◆ Include the rough draft grade as one category in the rubric of the finished product, perhaps as much as 10% of the final grade. You may also wish to include a category called "proofreading" and one called "on time."

♦ Consider having students edit or proofread with teacher assistance, so parents, other teachers, or advanced students (or exchange students) don't help by practically rewriting it for the student.

♦ Let students know that you expect to see improvement by making that an element of their grade.

USING FEEDBACK

Because writing is a continuous process, brainstorming, rough draft, revisions, and feedback are especially important to incorporate in writing assessment. Figure 4.1 (p. 62) is a form that I developed to provide students with feedback on errors made, so that corrections may be done. I like using this form because, instead of fixing students' errors, the students are merely given some guidance as to what sort of error was made, and they have to actively evaluate what they wrote (making it less likely that they will repeat the same error). This form also cuts in half (or more) the time it takes me to evaluate the effort, now that I am familiar with the symbols.

Another writing evaluation form and set of symbols may be found on the Internet at www.writekey.com, which uses a full credit, half credit, and no credit system. It was developed for use in foreign languages.

Some foreign language departments develop an all-purpose Writing Performance Rubric for use on all written performances. Figure 4.2 (p. 63) is an example of the Glendale Union School District's current rubric sheet, which is given to all teachers and students. It is reprinted here with permission from Vernon Jacobs.

Don't forget other sources such as the Internet, where the TOEFL (English as a Foreign Language) writing prompt may be found, as well as the Advanced Placement (AP) rubric that is used to grade foreign language compositions. Also, some foreign language catalogs offer feedback forms for purchase.

Feedback is sometimes positive (e.g., right, correct, good work, excellent analysis) but using only praise can be counterproductive. Using negative feedback (as in pointing out errors) can be and is useful if delivered in an objective and constructive manner, and delivered as soon as possible after the performance.

(Text continues on page 64.)

FIGURE 4.1 SELF-CORRECTING WRITING GUIDE: FRENCH

Articles	Nouns/ Pronouns	Adjectives	Verbs	Other
	4 Errors in: (A) gender (B) number (C) irregular plural	**9** BANGS error; most adjectives follow nouns, except for beauty/ age/number/ goodness/size	**13** Subject/verb agreement	**19** Spelling error
1 Needs article: (A) definite (B) indefinite (C) partitive (D) possessive (E) demonstrative (F) interrogative	**5** Dictionary error based on wrong part of speech.	**10** Irregular adjective: *eux > euse* *if > ive* and others…	**14** Negatives: *ne + verb + pas,* *ne + aux. verb + pas + past participle*	**20** Accent mark missing or incorrect
2 Preposition needs to form contraction: (A) *à > au, aux* (B) *de > du, des*	**6** Needs a direct object pronoun: *le, la, l', les me, te, nous, vous, se*	**11** Adjective agreement: add -e for fem. -s for plural	**15** (A) wrong tense (B) wrong mode	**21** Omit this word. See me if you don't know why.
3 Article not necessary after *pas* or *en*	**7** Needs an indirect object pronoun: *me, te, lui, se, nous, vous, leur*	**12** *C'est/il est* error. *C'est* + noun *il/elle est* + adj.	**16** Past tense: (A) avoir/etre problem (B) wrong past participle	**22** Word is English, not French.
	8 Use "que" to join 2 clauses		**17** Verb is followed by *à* or *de*	**23** A word is missing here.
			18 2nd verb doesn't get endings! (Use an infinitive here)	

FIGURE 4.2 FOREIGN LANGUAGE WRITING PERFORMANCE RUBRIC

Purpose:
1. The writing performance rubric is used to evaluate samples of written communicative skills.
2. It can be easily applied to any sample of extended written communication. The criteria of "Organization" necessitates more than a simple one sentence response.

Design: the assessment design requires that the student
1. write a composition in the target language in ink of at least:
   - 75 words for first year
   - 100 words for second year
   - 150 words for third year
   - 200 words for fourth year
2. address the prompt provided which is designed to elicit the contextual topic and grammatical structures of the current chapter or unit.

Further enhancements:
1. The student can be required to highlight the current chapter's:
   - vocabulary and expressions
   - grammatical structures
2. The student can use the rubric to analyze his sample and self-evaluate.
3. A "rough draft" may first be required for indication of errors. When returned to the student, he can indicate corrections and resubmit for enhancement of his grade.
4. The rubric provides a standard that can be used in cooperative group evaluation of others' rough or final drafts.

	Outstanding	Highly Successful	Successful	Not Yet Successful
Communication	For the level of study, the written response is: • predominantly comprehensible • appropriate • varied in detail	• comprehensible for the most part • appropriate • somewhat detailed	• generally comprehensible • appropriate • limited or repetitious in detail	• incomprehensible *or* • inappropriate *or* • inadequate
Accuracy of Written Language: Demonstrates control of: • spelling, capitalization and punctuation • verb tense(s) • word order and sentence structure • level appropriate grammar	The writing sample contains: • highly proficient and accurate language usage and is • virtually free of significant errors	• proficient and accurate language usage and may have • occasional significant errors	• predictable usage errors *that do not* • interfere with comprehension	• inadequate usage *or* • excessive errors *or is* • difficult to comprehend
Organization	The writing sample: • is logical and well ordered • flows smoothly throughout • has varied transitions	• is logical and well ordered • flows smoothly most of the time • has varied transitions	• is generally logical and organized *but* • may lack flow	• is illogical *or* • disorganized

Courtesy of Glendale Union School District, Glendale AZ

One good adjustment to make may be to get rid of your red pen. By the time students reach age 14 they look only for the red marks, note how many there are, and tend either to ignore the corrections or to react negatively to them. Try using a different color. For example, some teachers prefer to color-code their feedback: yellow highlighter for verbs, pink for gender, and green for usage.

Feedback sources do not have to be limited to the teacher. Students can self-evaluate the content and structure of their work, if not the grammatical accuracy. Peers can evaluate the accuracy and readability. Some languages, especially Spanish, may have access to a spell-checking or similar program if using a computer.

HOLISTIC RUBRIC

Figure 4.3 is a very simple holistic rubric to use for short writings, such as a riddle, metaphor, or anything about a paragraph in length.

FIGURE 4.3 A SIMPLE RUBRIC FOR SHORT WRITINGS
---

4   Well written. Good grammar; understandable use of language.

3   Language used accurately but no variety of usage.

2   Made several major errors in language, but essentially still understandable.

1   Made an effort but really didn't understand the assignment and/or many errors make it hard to understand.

POINT-BASED RUBRIC

Figure 4.4 is a form of analytical rubric. Analytical rubrics are such as this are probably the most commonly used.

Of course, when the rubric is presented, students will need examples to demonstrate the difference between, for instance, a 15-point content paper and a 5-point one. They will also want to know what an A, B, and so on grade is out of 50 points. So, the rubric is not as complete as could be desired.

FIGURE 4.4 COMMONLY USED ANALYTICAL RUBRIC

---

15 pts.	content and understandability
15 pts.	variety (sentence structure and vocabulary), accuracy (spelling, grammar)
10 pts.	objectives (i.e., length, creativity) met, as specified in product descriptor
10 pts.	editing (rough draft accompanies original) and met deadline for submitting draft
Total:	50 points

WRITING ACTIVITIES SAMPLES AND RUBRICS

Los Cuentos de Hadas is an example of a point-based project that was provided by Kathleen Sweeney Bulger of Cadillac High School in Cadillac, MI. This writing project is a year-end demonstration of mastery of two verb tenses, preterit and imperfect, which she got from the German teacher at her school and adapted/added to it to fit her own needs. She adds the following comments: "We do most of the work in class, so as to avoid any 'cheating' that might go on. The rough draft is turned in with the final draft, which should not be much different from the rough."

LOS CUENTOS DE HADAS (FAIRY TALES): ESPANOL 2

You will create a "fairy" tale in Spanish. The final project will be due ¡24 mayo 1999!

◆ Basic Requirements

- Must be written en español.

- Must use the Preterite and Imperfect throughout.

- Must be illustrated and typed.

- All work *must be original.*

- Books must have cover stating the title and author.

- Book must include dedication and at the end of the story a photo and a note about the author.

- Must be typewritten.

◆ In addition, you must include at *least* 9 of the following:

- Some kind of magic (i.e. magical numbers),

- One character who is especially pretty and good,

- Punishment because one does not do his duty/job,

- A curse,

- Transformation into an animal/object,

- A secret,

- A task to complete,

- A trip with difficulties,

- Animals, creatures, objects that speak,

- Good and bad wishes will be fulfilled,

- Someone is saved through the good deed of another,

- "Good" people have good luck, and

- *Required:* A happy and appropriate ending.

  All rough drafts must be turned in with the final draft!!!

Contributed by Kathleen Sweeney Bulger

Kathleen's rubric for this assignment is a simple, point-based one:

20 pts. Work done in class, on task

25 pts. Mechanics: grammar, spelling, sentence structure

10 pts. Originality/creativity

25 pts. Storyline, characterization, use of the required "ingredients"

10 pts. Dedication/author

10 pts. Neatness/illustrations

JOURNAL WRITING

Journal writing is commonly used, especially in upper-level foreign language classrooms. Journal writing is usually done a specified number of times per week, with a specified length for an acceptable entry. Some teachers assign a prompt, or topic. Others merely require that a variety of topics be used over several weeks' time. Most teachers read and respond to the journal entry, without being too concerned with correcting grammar and spelling, in the interests of using writing to communicate. For this reason, journals tend to have slightly different rubrics. Figure 4.5 is a sample product descriptor.

FIGURE 4.5 JOURNAL WRITING PRODUCT DESCRIPTOR

You will keep a personal journal in the folder provided, writing at least one page, single-spaced each week in French. A journal is a reflection on a topic such as (but not limited to):

♦ My weekend

♦ My favorite (i.e., film, music, artist, class, food, shirt)

♦ Pet peeves

♦ Pets or family members

♦ News items

♦ Sports and teams

It is *not* a list. All entries should be in complete sentences. No English words may be used: you should *try* to write without using a dictionary, and must underline all words you looked up.

Figure 4.6 is a very good holistic rubric to use for grading journals.

FIGURE 4.6 HOLISTIC RUBRIC TO GRADE JOURNALS

Excellent 9–10 pts.
- Includes specific details of personal thoughts or feelings
- Shows evidence of reflection and introspection
- Addresses all aspects of the writing prompt
- Neatly written and legible

Good 7–8 pts.
- Includes general details of personal thought or feelings
- Shows reflection and introspection
- Attempts most aspects of the writing prompt
- Legible

Fair 5–6 pts.
- Includes only limited expansion of ideas
- Shows some evidence of reflection
- Omits one or more aspects of the writing prompt
- Rather difficult to read

Marginal 3–4 pts.
- Responds in short, superficial manner Includes no evidence of reflection
- Does not correspond to prompt
- Almost illegible

Failing 0 pt.
- No entry

NAME POEMS

This is a short, creative way to use adjectives, and to check for correct gender. It is a high-interest activity, so be sure to post the students' poems for the other students to read!

NAME POEMS

Instructions:

Use your first and last names to creative a vertical adjective poem that describes you. You must:

◆ Call attention to the letters of your name (i.e., bigger, different color);

◆ Write your name so the letters line up vertically;

◆ Make adjectives agree with your own gender; and

◆ Write or type it large enough to be easily read from several feet away.

Example (in English):

Divine

Enthusiastic

Bookish

(notice that the letters can be inside a word that describes you ☺)

su**B**tle

Lively

cre**A**tive

cra**Z**y

Rubric

Criteria	Excellent 4–5 pt.	Acceptable 3 pt.	Unacceptable 1–2 pt.
Visual	• vertical adjectives • letters highlighted • describes you well • neat creative • well-designed	• vertical adjectives • letters highlighted • describes you well	• requirements not met
Grammar and Spelling	• all words spelled correctly • uses correct adjective agreement	• all words spelled correctly • uses correct adjective agreement	• requirements not met
Time	• handed in on time	• handed in on time	• requirements not met

The poem in Figure 4.7 received a 5 (A). It easily fits the descriptions under Excellent.

FIGURE 4.7 NAME POEM: SUZANNE

The poem in Figure 4.8 received a 2 (D). It is not done neatly and it contains errors. I did give the student a break because French doesn't have many "K" words in it.

FIGURE 4.8 NAME POEM: ERIKA

Sportiv **E**

Rollerblading   ) Not an adjective
                           Not in French!

pol **I** e

Ce wee **K** end   ) Not an adjective,
                            but good try!

A chats   ) Not an
                           adjective!

D
Too many errors
No color used
Not creative!

PERSONIFICATION

Choose an object from this chapter. Pretend that you are this object and write for it, describing the following: your family, your likes and dislikes, and your favorite things to do. Find a picture to scan to add to your composition. We will go to the Cyber Station to scan your picture and type your final draft. You need a minimum of 20 sentences. Here is the rubric for grading this project:

An "A" paper	A "B" paper	A "C" paper	A "D" paper	An "F" paper
• in 1st person	• in 1st person	• in 1st person	• in 1st person	• is not in the 1st person
• describes family	• describes family	• describes family	• does not contain one of the required categories	• does not contain two of the required categories
• describes things to do	• describes things to do	• describes things to do	• is at least 15 sentences	• is less than 15 sentences
• describes likes and dislikes	• describes likes and dislikes	• describes likes and dislikes	• has no picture	• has many errors in spelling and/or grammar
• is at least 20 sentences	• is at least 18 sentences	• is at least 18 sentences	• has more than 5 spelling errors	• is not completely in French
• has a picture	• has a picture	• has a picture	• has no organization	
• is spelled correctly	• is spelled correctly	• has a few spelling errors	• has more than 5 grammar errors	
• is logically organized in paragraphs	• is logically organized in paragraphs	• is not organized by topic		
• uses correct grammar	• uses correct grammar	• has few grammar errors		
• is creative				

IF I WERE

This activity is done after presenting the conditional tense and reading the poem "Ah, si j'étais!…" by Catherine Rihoit, found in the text *En Bonne Forme*. Because the purpose of this writing is to show mastery of this verb tense, it is stressed more than usual in the rubric.

IF I WERE

You will write 10 sentences beginning with "Si j'étais...." As in the poem, you must use

a famous person	an adjective
a fictional character	a person of the opposite sex
a geographical feature	a plant
an animal	an element

The final two may be your choice. By reading your poem, I should glean an idea of your interests, politics, and your hopes for the future.

Here is the rubric that will be used:

An "A" poem will have:	A "B" poem will have:	A "C" poem will have:	Unacceptable:
• correct grammar and spelling • shows politics and future hopes • easily understood by any audience	• one or two spelling errors • no political view • an unclear sense of the author's personality	• a verb written incorrectly • ideas expressed in an unclear fashion • vocabulary used incorrectly	• less than 10 sentences • missing any of the eight required elements • uses English words • late

The work in Figure 4.9 received a "B/C" (like a B– or C+). All the verbs were correct, but there were several fairly big errors involved: nothing really political, the "invincible" rather than "invisible" man, with a failed attempt to say that no one could see them, and the incorrect usage of "embarrassée" for embarrassed. Although there were several striking images, the poem had a disjointed feel, sometimes wanting to move, and sometimes wanting to stop.

FIGURE 4.9 EXAMPLE 1: A B/C GRADE

Si j'étais Edgar Allan Poe, j'écrirais beaucoup de poèmes morbides.

Si j'étais Hillary Clinton, je serais très embarrassée et honteuse de mon mari.

Si j'étais Giles Cory, je me croirais obligée de parler plus tôt en faveur des innocents.

Si j'étais L'Homme Invincible, je ne verrais personne.

Si j'étais Robin Williams, je serais très drôle.

Si j'étais une falaise, je dirais à tout le monde de sauter de mon bord.

Si j'étais un oiseau, je volerais dans le monde entier.

Si j'étais une porte, je me fermerais sur tout le monde.

Si j'étais le temps, j'arrêterais pour des siècles à un temps.

Si j'étais une orage, je serais contente.

The poem in Figure 4.10 received an A. There were virtually no errors, all the required elements were present, and the poem has a unity of thought, evidence of some cultural knowledge, and would be easily understood.

FIGURE 4.10 EXAMPLE 2: AN A GRADE

Si j'étais colonel, je n'irais pas à la guerre.

Si j'étais Clinton, je ne dirais rien aux journalistes.

Si j'étais Sleeping Beauty, je tournerais ma joue pour ne pas recevoir le baiser du prince.

Si j'étais Emily Dickinson, je n'écrirais pas au monde.

Si j'étais Albert Einstein, j'étudierais la littérature.

Si j'étais Elizabeth I d'Angleterre, je naviguerais des bateaux au Nouveau Monde.

Si j'étais un caillou, je voyagerais beaucoup.

Si j'étais un dauphin, je ne parlerais pas aux hommes.

Si j'étais riche, je donnerais l'argent aux pauvres.

Si j'étais pauvre, je serais, pour la première fois peut-être, contente.

PERSONALIZED ESSAY

The following example of a final exam writing assessment, a personalized essay, and with rubrics and student samples, was generous submitted by Kimberly Kaufman of Cambridge, Massachusetts. She also sent this explanation:

> Our department (Classical and Modern Languages) developed these [rubrics] by working closely with other school systems who already had rubrics in place. Ours were developed about four years ago and are in a constant state of revision. We use them for *all* assessment in the department, although some teachers have developed rubrics more specifically geared toward assessment of oral performance. …We use our rubrics to assess skits, projects, "objective" tests, quizzes and exams, compositions, and other oral work.
>
> It is a learning process to use them correctly. Often it is easier to begin by using them for grading compositions and monologues, and then expand to using them for exams, as the exams must be scored

holistically rather than by the traditional point system. We spend one or two days a year in language-specific groups grading tapes and compositions to make sure that we're consistent across the department in our use of the rubrics.

I have included some sample compositions [Figures 4.13, p. 80, 4.14, p. 81, and 4.15, p. 82] from the mid-year exams written by students in Spanish I.

The rubric in Figure 4.11 (p. 77) was developed by these Wellesley High School (Wellesley, MA) staff members: Richard Deppe; Sue DiGiandomenico; Paul Esposito; Mary Gottschalk; Mim Grodberg; Peter Haggerty; Kim Kaufman; Jim Kelleher; Christine Laborde-Castérot; Susan Moore; Lynn Moore-Benson; and Marlies Stueart.

The explanation in Figure 4.12 (p. 78), written by Richard Deppe, is used to inform students, parents, and guidance counselors about the department's grading procedures and philosophy.

FIGURE 4.11 RUBRIC FOR HOLISTIC SCORING

<u>5 (A)</u>   [Demonstrates excellence]

The student demonstrates a strong command of the language through excellent control of complex stuctures, idioms, and general vocabulary. The student's message is very effectively communicated. Required responses are provided in an appropriate and creative fashion through thematic development. There are almost no significant errors.

<u>4 (B)</u> [Demonstrates good command with only limited difficulties]

The student demonstrates consistently good use of the language. He/She shows good control of elementary structures and suggests understanding of more complex. His/Her message expressed is generally comprehended by the listener. Vocabulary is used coherently. The student makes appropriate use of circumlocution (*i.e.* vocabulary and expressions that are less appropriate and direct, but still communicate an intelligible and suitable answer). There are a few significant errors and some awkwardness of expression.

<u>3 (C)</u> [Demonstrates adequate command with some weaknesses]

The student demonstrates acceptable use of the language. The message is comprehensible, although difficult, at times, to follow. The use of vocabulary is appropriate but limited and there is occasional interference from vocabulary of the student's native language. In writing there are some significant spelling errors. Occasionally; there are serious grammatical errors that interfere with comprehension. In oral work the student's pronunciation shows sufficient deviation from that of a native speaker so that occasional confusion results on the part of the listener.

<u>2 (D)</u> [Falls below expectations]

The message is communicated with difficulty and is unclear. There are numerous errors in word order and forms, along with inappropriate or quite limited use of vocabulary and idiomatic structures. In oral work the student's pronunciation shows dramatic deviation from that of a native speaker so that frequent confusion and lack of comprehension result on the part of the listener.
There is little evidence that the student meets minimal expectations.

<u>1 (F)</u> [Unacceptable]

The student demonstrates clear lack of competence. The message communicated is barely intelligible or not at all. There is little or no sense of word order and forms. Vocabulary is repetitive, extremely limited, and inadequate. In oral work the student demonstrates no ability to mirror, even on the most basic level, the pronunciation of a native speaker. There is virtually no comprehension on the part of the listener.

Contributed by Kimberly Kaufman.

FIGURE 4.12 EXPLANATION OF GRADING

Rubrics: In all foreign language courses rubrics have been or are being developed that are designed to give students more detailed and specific information regarding performance in reading, writing, and, where applicable, speaking and listening. The grades students receive refer to their level of proficiency in accordance with these rubrics, and are designated by the numbers 1, 2, 3, 4, and 5, with 5 being the highest. In all instances, save the midyear and final examinations, the addition of a plus or minus to these grades is possible and such indicates a student's proficiency that is slightly above or below the rubric score *per se*. Percentage grading, reflecting quantity and not quality, is therefore not needed nor used.

Sequential Grading: The nature of study and mastery in virtually all foreign language courses is such that a student is required constantly both to retain all materials learned from the onset of study and to build upon these to achieve greater mastery of all elements of the language. For this reason, the department believes that for us the averaging of grades over the course of the year makes little sense. As an illustration let us consider the following sets of grades: A [at the end of the first quarter], C [at the midyear], F [at the end of year] for student one, and the reverse for student two [*viz.* F, C, and A]. The averages in both instances would be about a C, yet it is obvious that student two is penalized for such an averaging, as he or she has actually mastered virtually all of the material by the end of the year, and student one would be shown to be in average control of the materials, whereas in truth he or she has substandard control. With the process of sequential grading such inequities are righted. Student one would receive a grade below C and student two would receive a grade above C. This system is not only fairer in the case of sequential courses such as ours, but also offers constant encouragement to students to try their best and improve, for their efforts will be rewarded. Conversely, it penalizes students who perform well at the outset and then choose to rest upon their laurels with the expectation that their earlier achievement will preclude a failing grade in the course.

Questions regarding either of these Classical and Modern Language Department policies may be directed to the department head.

Contributed by Kimberly Kaufman.

On the following pages are excerpted examples of student work. The student who wrote essay #1 (Figure 4.13, page 80) received a "2" (falls below expectations). Teacher Kim Kaufman explained the score as follows: "[The student] generally followed the instructions, but left out some information, and did not reach the required 35 sentences for Level 1. Use of the language is comprehensible, with some spelling errors and errors in agreement. This might have received a "3" if the essay had been the appropriate length."

The student who wrote essay #2 (Figure 4.14, page 81) received a "5" (demonstrates excellence in achieving expectations). Here is teacher Kim Kaufman's explanation for this score: "This student wrote an essay of the appropriate length and included all the required information. She shows high ability in use of the verb *gustar* and range of vocabulary. She does have some errors (. . . *y inteligente . . .*), but this grammar rule had not yet been covered in class. I believe this is a representative essay of just about the best we can expect from a beginning language student in her first semester."

The student who wrote essay #3 (Figure 4.15, page 82) received a "4" (meets expectations with limited problems). Kim Kaufman: "This student has some signs of sophistication (*Si you tengo dinero suficiente yo quiero comprar dos o tres discos compactos para ella o una camisa roja proque a ella le gustan mucho las cosas rojas*), but also has quite a few spelling and agreement errors (*las cosas rojo*) and interference with other languages."

FIGURE 4.13 ASSESSMENT MODEL: ESSAY #1(EXCERPT)

Part IV - Writing (25% of exam)

You are going to your best friend's 15th birthday party next week. Your friend has told you all about her plans for the party. Imagine you have a pen pal in Spain whom you write to regularly. Write him a letter telling him about your plans for the party. In your letter you should include the following information and questions but you may also include anything else you think of as well. You should have at least 20 sentences if you are in level 3 or the middle school, 25 for level 2, and 35 for level 1. Your paragraph should use the present tense, Ir+A+ Infinitive , and present progressive. Include as many details as you are able to. Remeber to include colors and numbers in your description.

Bien

Tell him........
-who the party is for
-when (date and time) and where it will take place
-who will be there
-what you will do at the party.
-explain how people will dress
-what you will wear and ask his advice
-ask what you should give her and give your ideas
-what you will eat
-ask him if he is going to any parties soon?

Yo voy a assistir fiesta.

Include cultural references that you learned about the *Quinceañera* on the internet.

Hola!

Yo voy fiesta. En La fiesta es en el dia trace de Noviembre, en Sabado, Son las ocho de la Noche. Es fiesta Para (for) mi Amiga Ana. Yo voy a comer la comida Italiana y la comida papas fritas. Yo voy a jugar video juegos en la fiesta. Yo voy a hablar can mi Amigos en la fiesta. Yo voy quiero comprar muchos ropas para ella cumpleaños fiesta. Yo voy En la fiesta la ropas

---

Contributed by Kimberly Kaufman.

FIGURE 4.14 ASSESSMENT MODEL: ESSAY #2 (EXCERPT)

A la vesta, vamos a comer mucha comida buena. Por exemplo, pizza, fruta, la comida mexicana, el chocolate, y más. Tambien, vamos a bailar y Ana va a recibir regalos. ¡Ay no! ¿Yo necèsito comprar un regalo para Ana! ¿Qué le gusta a Ana? Voy a comprar zapatillos de tenis para Ana, porque le gustan los deportes mucho - ¿Qué piensas? Pienso que zapatillas de tenis son un regalo muy bueno ¿Verdad?

Contributed by Kimberly Kaufman.

FIGURE 4.15 ASSESSMENT MODEL: ESSAY #3 (EXCERPT)

negro. ¿Y tu? ¿cuale camiza vas tu poner?
Ahora yo no sais cuales regalos para comprar para
ella. Yo no sais que quieres. No es facilidede de
comprar cosas para una chica. ¿Y tu, que vas tu a
comprar para ella? Ci yo tengo dinero sufficiente,
 yo quero comprar dos o tres discos compaticos
para ella o una camiza rojo porque ella le
gusta mucho a los cosas rojo. Es el color
favorita de Juanita.

La restaurante es una restaurante
muy bueno con la comida fenomenal. Tu
quero comer el pollo o una hambergexa con papas
fritas.

¿Tu vas a una fiesta esta semana? ¿Que tu
haces para Nova Anos "la, nochevieja"? Mi telephoner quando
tu sabe o va ser una fiesta ok? Tengo
que irme. ¡Adiós!

Contributed by Kimberly Kaufman.

5

FROM THEORY TO PRACTICE: READING ASSESSMENTS

The following list is a fairly complete summary of activities ordinarily used for reading performance assessments:

advertisement	metaphor	reading log
book jacket	mind map	retelling
book report	mock interview	script
critique/review	monologue	Socratic seminar
discussion	newscast	storyboard
game rules	new story ending	time line
K-W-L sheet	order blank	travel log
journal	outline	Venn diagram
map	poster	video

Reading is primarily a receptive skill, so converting a reading activity to a performance assessment is difficult. Standard methods of assessment, such as true/false, matching, cloze activities, fill-in-the-blank, or short answers to questions at the end of the selection or chapter, are not true performance assessments, of course. However, because reading is primarily a mental activity, we assess reading primarily by having students produce a spoken or written product, and therefore you can probably find rubrics in the chapters on oral and written assessments that would work to assess reading as well.

We should also remind ourselves that all reading does not involve literature. Textbooks provide reading materials in many shapes and forms: advertisements, menus, cartoons, headlines and news stories, dialogues, poems, and short stories in storyboard and standard form, as well as longer selections of "real literature" in upper-level texts. Students of all levels of language are, and should be, regularly asked to read in the target language.

SELF-ASSESSMENT

What assessment method is used depends in great part on what skills you wish to assess, and who is doing the assessing. If the student is doing the assessing, the student usually rates him- or herself on a scale of Novice to Distinguished level, based on the criteria. On the next page is such a self-assessment.

TEACHER ASSESSMENT

Teachers, however, do most assessments. One performance assessment method often used by teachers *while students are reading* is a basic observation checklist. This identifies the behaviors the teacher wishes to observe students doing, and provides a space for the observer to record how often this behavior is observed. Some common reading activities that are observable are:

- ◆ Scanning to find information before reading;
- ◆ Scanning to find information while reading;
- ◆ Using various cues for word meaning in context;
- ◆ Keeping a list of key words;
- ◆ Underlining familiar words or a particular verb tense;
- ◆ Looking up unfamiliar words in a dictionary;
- ◆ Making an outline or graphic organizer while reading; and
- ◆ Underlining the main point or most important information.

Because many students have poor reading skills, we who are foreign language teachers often have to teach them (and require them) to use good reading practices. Examples include asking the students to look at the illustration provided with the reading selection and write down many things they might expect to find in the selection, based upon that illustration. Another good tactic is to ask them to scan through the selection to locate and underline words they already know (which, if there are many, would considerably reduce their anxiety about the length of the reading selection), or words that occur many times (which may be key and can be looked up before beginning the reading), or to underline a certain verb tense (which would highlight a grammatical point that the selection is intended to portray, such as a short story that illustrates the various uses of the imperfect tense, or the contrast between the imperfect and the

ASSESS YOUR READING PROFICIENCY

Get a copy of a current newspaper and read it as much as you can.

Check what you have read with a reader skilled in this language who has read the same selection.

Decide as honestly as possible which of these categories you fit in:

- *Novice A*—I can only identify a word here or there.

- *Novice B*—I can identify words based on their relationship to English and pictures, but have to reread them to be certain.

- *Novice C*—I can read phrases and expressions such as items on menus, schedules, maps and signs, but not every time.

- *Intermediate A*—I can understand the main idea of a selection (i.e. headlines).

- *Intermediate B*—I can read simple descriptions of people, places or things when it is a topic I am already familiar with (i.e. a description of a movie I have seen).

- *Intermediate C*—I can read a news story about an event and summarize what I have read, but not give details on everything that happened.

- *Advanced A*—I can read a story, and retell it in detail (who, what, when, where, etc.) accurately.

- *Advanced B*—I can read an editorial or political commentary and understand it, along with some of the cultural knowledge it requires.

preterit—in French, the passé composé—or, in German, because the two portions of a past tense verb are usually in different parts of the sentence, underlining them will make them easier for a beginning-level reader to find the whole verb while reading).

After having read Stephen Krashen's considerable evidence on the value of free reading in language acquisition, I keep a set of children's books in my classroom, and give students 15 minutes or so to read a book of their choice, while I walk around and observe. Of course, I share this checklist with students before they begin the reading, so that they know what behaviors I would expect to see. Figure 5.1 is a checklist form that I have used at Level 2 for evaluating students during a period of free reading.

FIGURE 5.1 FREE READING TIME

STUDENT	Reads without talking to others	Keeps list of new words learned	Writes down words to look up

TYPES OF ACTIVITIES

Most reading assessments, however, are done after a reader has stopped reading, either partially through or at the end of a reading selection. Then, a performance/product is expected from the reader. The list of reading assessment activities at the beginning of this chapter enables a student to demonstrate his or her ability to process what was read, to identify topics covered in the item read, and to demonstrate his or her perception of it and opinions about it by producing a variety of performances as evidence. The activities can be divided according to the type of behavior required of the student, as follows:

Organize	*Demonstrate*	*Process*	*Create*
K-W-L chart	ad	discussion	book jacket
job application	critique/review	journal	game
map	mock interview	retelling	letter
mind map	monologue	script	metaphor
outline	newscast	Socratic seminar	new ending
storyboard	newspaper		updated version
time line	order blank		video
travel log	poster		
Venn diagram	report		

For the rest of this chapter, I will take these activities, column by column, and explain and illustrate some of these performance assessments.

ORGANIZING INFORMATION THAT IS READ

SCAFFOLDING

A key reading strategy that we must teach students is "scaffolding." In scaffolding, students learn to visually represent information that they find in a reading selection. There are many types of scaffolding. I use authentic activities listed in specific situations. For example, if we are reading the want ads, I have students fill out a job application for one of the positions. They would need to locate, in the reading, and transfer to the application, information such as the employer's name, location, and phone number, as well as the required skills, work hours, and so on. A job application could become a creative activity, however, if you have the student pretend to be a character from a story or poem read, and have them apply to be a teacher, doctor, politician, or whatever, listing skills, job experience, or whatever.

I use a map when we are reading about a vacation, covering a novel in which the character travels from place to place (e.g., *Candide, Don Quixote, Steppenwolf*), or when reading historical selections. This helps students both picture events, and firmly fix in their minds the order in which they happened.

A mind map (there are many other names for this) is another form of graphic organizer that students fill out while reading, and that helps to list data from the reading so that it is more easily accessible to them for a later discussion, composition, or creative performance. Figure 5.2 is an example of a graphic organizer that we use when reading a short story. I evaluate these maps on a pass/fail basis (they must be completely filled out) as I use them as a stepping stone to a later activity. It is very similar to an outline, and easier to use.

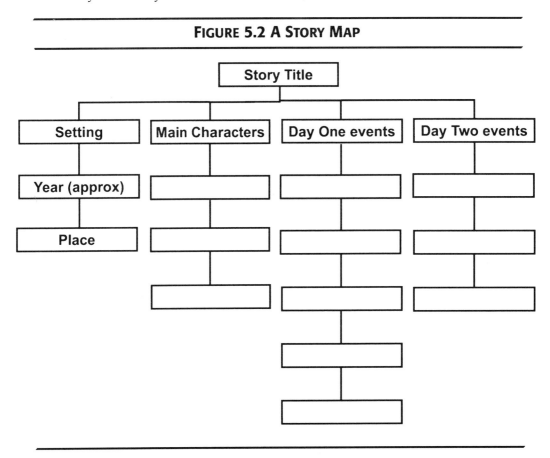

FIGURE 5.2 A STORY MAP

STORYBOARD

A storyboard leads quite nicely into a speaking activity, and is easier for students to do in classes using a TPRS format (which focuses on oral production of language). As students read a story or story-poem, they draw the events into a sort of cartoon form, using which they can then show and "read" to a classmate or teacher for an assessment, or, if a variety of stories are being read, exchange it with classmates who might then write questions about the story they are given, or attempt to tell it to the student who read the story (a great opportunity for that student to be an "expert" on his or her story, a great confidence-builder.) A storyboard would make students focus on such aspects as the setting of events, actions taken, and how a character looks, which are all key aspects of a reading selection.

TIME LINE

A time line is just what it sounds like. Students draw a line and list events on it as they occur. Then they have a graphic representation of historical events, a character's life history, or a sequence of steps needed for a procedure (if, for example, you are reading a recipe or doing a sewing or construction project). These should be evaluated on how complete they are. I suggest showing students several time lines, and having them help you decide which one is best and why. List those characteristics of the best one, and you have your product descriptor and a list of what an "A" time line should have.

CREATIVE ACTIVITIES TO SHOW UNDERSTANDING OF WHAT WAS READ

♦ Interview: Students each play a character, and are interviewed by classmates (provided with questions by the student), and all take notes.

♦ Write a letter of recommendation for a fictional character in a story.

♦ Venn diagram: Using interlocking circles, compare and contrast two characters. One character is represented by one circle, and the second circle represents the other character. Anything they have in common goes in the section where the circles overlap.

♦ Explain what problem a character faced and how it was resolved.

♦ Retell a story in your own words.

♦ For every action in a story, list the motivation/reason it occurred.

♦ Write a newscast about the events taking place in the book/story.

♦ Write a different ending for the story.

♦ Critique the story. How could the author have done it differently? Better?

- Give a personal response to literature (e.g., How did this story change your ideas [or add to your understanding] about _____? Explain your response using ideas from the story as well as your own experience.) Use this as a good journal topic (see Chapter 4 on journal writing).

- Poetry: Analyze the imagery in a poem by drawing a picture that shows what you have read. Compare your picture with those of your classmates.

- Analyze the figures of speech used in a poem, and write some poems of your own.

- Advertisements: Evaluate the claims made in an advertisement.

- Analyze how the advertisement uses persuasion.

- Write an advertisement and perform it; feature a catchy slogan in your advertisement.

6

FROM THEORY TO PRACTICE: ASSESSMENTS OF LISTENING PROFICIENCY

Listening is a complex skill that involves knowledge of vocabulary, grammar (i.e., verb endings), and culture (i.e., formal and informal situations), and an ability to put what is heard into context and react to it. Training students to listen is one of the harder things foreign language teachers do.

I like to use the metaphor of running on a riverbank, speaking to someone in a boat. You cannot stop running, because the person on the boat will move out of range; you can't stop the boat every time you hear a word you don't know; and you can't fixate on just one word, or you won't hear the rest of the message. You also will not have time to translate everything into English, because you will slow too much to keep up with the boat. This is one "picture" I present to students, with the message that listening is a learned skill, not to give up but "go with the flow," and that success lies in learning how to listen.

A second bit of advice is from brain research: The brain can process information much faster than anyone can speak. This means that, as you listen, you have plenty of time to repeat (silently, to yourself) what you hear the person saying. This should help your brain process oral input and give you a mental "big picture" image of what is being said.

CONSTRUCTING A LISTENING ACTIVITY

There are several steps involved in choosing the correct type of listening activity for assessment. The first is to choose the purpose: academic or real-life simulation. Then, choose the listening stimulus: Monologue or dialogue? Au-

91

dio only? Video only? Audio + static visual? Video + computer? Then, determine a compatible response formula as shown in Figure 6.1.

FIGURE 6.1 RESPONSE FORMULA BASED ON PURPOSE

Academic responses	*Realistic responses*
Point exercises: checklist, visual identification	Respond orally
Complete open-ended statements	State main idea (gist)
Dictation	Paraphrase
Fill in information grid with main ideas	Summarize/condense
Cloze (fill in missing words)	Act out response
Content question/answer	Transfer to another skill (take message, fill out form)
Think aloud, written reflection	Converse

USING TAPES FOR LISTENING ASSESSMENTS

Unfortunately, most tests provided by our texts provide an easily-scored listening section that either requires students to match a taped dialogue with an appropriate picture (matching) or to choose the appropriate answer to a taped question, or complete a conversation (multiple choice).These are, however, fairly easy to adapt for a better listening activity. The best and most authentic method of assessing listening requires a student to provide some sort of response, either written or oral. Have students answer, either orally or in written form, the questions asked on the tape (instead of selecting an appropriate answer from a list). Have students listen to a brief conversation, and then describe it on a form that you provide to them.

Figure 6.2 is an example of the form (ordinarily, this form is in the target language, but I will show all examples in this chapter in English).

FIGURE 6.2 LISTENING ACTIVITY FORM

Listening Activity: Tape 1

Name_____

Speaker's names:_____ M ___ F___   Age (approx.) ____

_____ M ___ F___   Age (approx.) ____

Where they are: _____

Main topics of conversation: _____

_____

What will they do next? _____

To evaluate the listening activity form, I generally give either a participation grade if it is completely filled out, or else use a point system (e.g., the form in Figure 6.2 is worth 10 points as there are 10 different items of information for students to listen for). Figure 6.2 is used for a conversation on an audiotape. If it were a conversation on videotape, I would also ask students to provide information on the visual content of the presentation, usually cultural things such as gestures.

Another variation on this is to provide a visually interesting form for students to fill out, giving them a simulation-like role in the activity. This is limited only by your imagination. Here are some examples:

- The student is a police sketch artist, and completes a sketch of the person described.

- The student is a waiter, filling out a bill as the person on the tape orders.

- The student is a doctor, and completes a medical form as the patient provides information on their name, age, general health, and symptoms.

- The student is looking for an apartment, and takes down information that a potential landlord gives them.

- The student is an emergency worker who takes down information on an accident.

- The student is a grocer (or other type of merchant) who takes down the items ordered by a customer.

◆ The secretary/student takes down information for their boss from a telephone caller.

◆ As a person describes their family, the student fills out a family tree for that person.

◆ As a customer orders clothing, the listener fills out an order form.

◆ As a client describes to the student/mover how they would like the furniture placed in their new home, the student draws a diagram of the items (or draws arrows from pictures to the location, or moves and tapes down cut-out pictures to their correct places).

As simulations, many of the above are obviously good career simulations of actual jobs that students with a knowledge of the target language could perform or be asked to perform some day. Figure 6.3 is an example of a form to fill out for the customer ordering clothing example.

FIGURE 6.3 CUSTOMER ORDER FORM

Customer name_____

Address _____

Item number	Item name	Color	Size	How many	Cost each	Total cost

This method is, of course, only good if you have a good supply of taped conversations. Sometimes you may have to make your own tapes (or talk a native speaker into doing them for you). However, you will find that most of the testing tapes provided by your text are easily adaptable for this purpose; just don't provide the multiple-choice answers.

USING MANIPULATIVES FOR LISTENING ASSESSMENT

Not all types of assessments are used for unit tests, or finals. Daily assessments to ascertain student skill in listening are important as well. Easy examples of manipulative activities are types of "signaling" activities; for example, have students raise pink or blue pieces of paper to indicate they hear a masculine or feminine noun or adjective being used. Most of us use props such as clocks with hands for students to adjust to our specifications, number, or alphabet cards to hold above our heads, or whiteboards (which students write or draw on according to what they hear). A good source of whiteboard activities is my book *Foreign Language Teacher's Guide to Active Learning* (1999) or the archives of FL-TEACH.

I have one I like to use when teaching students to differentiate between the imperfect and preterit (passé composé) tenses. As I tell a story (sometimes a true one, other times a silly one), students listen and, if the verb is in the preterit, clap their hands (reinforcing that this is a single, finished action), but if the verb is imperfect, they drum their heels on the floor (for continuing past action).

A "Silent Auction" is another great manipulative activity for listening practice. I have students cut out pictures that illustrate chapter vocabulary (usually as homework). In class, I ask them for a series of items (in the target language, of course): "Show me a white refrigerator/flowered shirt/short blonde, blue-eyed girl with earrings/can of soup," and the first student (or group) to show me this item earns two points, with any others producing that item receiving one point. If working in groups, I deduct two points from the team score for any use of English. Keep the pace moving quickly, and the interest and participation levels will remain high. I have some sort of reward for the winner(s) at the end. Obviously, this can be used for any unit with large amounts of vocabulary. Good units to use this for include those on personal description, descriptions of objects (i.e., thick, smooth), foods, household items, sports, colors, and clothing. I have even used this for a chapter on adjectives (where they had to listen for the gender of the adjective as well as the word itself) and to practice verbs in a chapter with many new verbs. After the activity is over, turn the pictures into a mobile or a collage for the classroom walls, for more vocabulary practice.

USING PAIRED ACTIVITIES TO ASSESS LISTENING

Activities done with a partner will help students speak as well as listen. Many activities can be done with two people sitting back to back and conversing in the target language. Faces, Maps, and Battleship/Master Mind are three examples.

FACES

Have students fold a piece of paper into fourths. On the top two sections, have them draw faces as you describe them: "A round face with tiny eyes, a wide nose with freckles, and a big smile; long curly hair, an earring, and a scar on the forehead." On the third section have students draw their own face. For the fourth section, in pairs, they would then draw the face their partner describes to them. A hilarious variation on this is to have students place their paper on a book, and place the book on their head. Drawing without being able to see what is being drawn generates giggles during the process, and guffaws when they see their final product. It is still easy for them to tell if they drew the correct characteristics; in fact, they tend to comment (in the target language) more on what they have drawn.

MAPS

MAP ACTIVITY #1

Give students maps of the same city. Have them each pick a place on the map to begin (Point A) and a place to end (Point B), tracing the route between the two points in pencil or pen. Taking turns, students will give each other directions on how to get from Point A to Point B. If Student A is giving the directions, then Student B is tracing the route on his or her map. Staple both maps together; they should match perfectly.

MAP ACTIVITY #2

Give students maps of the same town, but each map has only half the sites labeled—Map A has the sites missing from Map B, and vice versa. Seated back to back, students take turns naming a site and describing its location, or listening to the description and marking that site on their map. Again, both maps should match exactly.

MAP ACTIVITY #3

Maps may also be used when learning place names and practicing giving directions. Again, each student would be given a map that has information not available to his or her partner. Have one student ask another what type of building is on the corner of First and Elm is, or how to get from Point A to a café.

BATTLESHIP/MASTER MIND

Any activity that could be converted into a grid format can be made into a fun activity patterned after a combination of the games Battleship and Master Mind. Using previously practiced vocabulary or grammar, have students construct a 3×3 or 4×4 grid similar to a bingo card, with verb forms or grammar words inserted where the numbers would be, and appropriate headings on the top and side of the grids: for example, use vocabulary such as colors, numbers, or days of the week. Also, give students a blank grid. Students take turns guessing the position of the various words/pronouns/verb forms. Have them take turns trying to figure out what and where their partner placed things by asking questions such as: "Is 'foot' at Sunday noon?" If the answer is yes, they write that on the blank grid, and get another turn ("Is 'head' at Sunday two o'clock?"). If the answer is no, then it is their partner's turn. The student who completes an accurate copy of his or her partner's grid first, wins.

(A lot of the activities from the Listening to Tapes section earlier in this chapter could be adapted as partner activities, as could many of the activities in Chapter 4.)

GRADING LISTENING ACTIVITIES

As stated previously, it depends on whether the activity is an assessment for purposes of review, determining whether students are ready for a test, or for actual testing purposes. Grades given can be pass/fail (e.g., No English used/English used, Tried it all/Incomplete) or using points, or a rubric similar to Figure 6.4 can be used.

FIGURE 6.4 RUBRIC FOR LISTENING ACTIVITIES

Excellent	Good	Needs Improvement
Completed entire activity	Completed most of activity	Completed less than 2/3 of activity
Required no repetition	Requested one repetition	Repeated repetitions necessary
No errors in written response	Few errors in written response	More than 3 errors in writing

7

STRATEGIES FOR KEEPING ASSESSMENTS MANAGEABLE

Teachers faced with the challenge of administering multiple assessments, especially performance assessments, always ask, "How do we find time to give and grade all these assessments?" I have no easy solution. Performance assessments and their rubrics do take time to create, and to grade. However, there are several easy ways to streamline your assessment procedure.

MAKE SURE THEY KNOW WHAT YOU WANT

The easiest way to make assessment easier is to develop general rubrics like those seen in earlier chapters, either departmentally, schoolwide, or system-wide, or use your state or national standards.

- ◆ Post them in the classroom.
- ◆ Discuss them.
- ◆ Review them frequently, before and after assessments.
- ◆ Use the criteria every time, not just occasionally.

If students know beforehand that you will grade using those criteria *every time* and they know the criteria well, they will attempt to satisfy those criteria. Again, letting students help you "grade" a couple of sample products will greatly increase their familiarity with and understanding of the rubric(s). Students, parents, and administrators will view the application of "writing" criteria that students are familiar with to any written product of theirs as "fair." Additionally, repeatedly using the same criteria will also increase your familiarity with them as well, making it easier for you to quickly scan a product for the necessary aspects.

ASSESS USING A "CLOZE" OR RANDOM METHOD

Collecting several pages of homework per day from students soon results in massive overload for a teacher, yet having students grade each other's papers often leads to cheating. Therefore, grade class work and homework on a random basis to streamline evaluations. In other words, the teacher selects just one section, or even the last few items of one section, to evaluate performance. For example, on a crossword, look to see if two or three difficult fill-ins were correctly performed. This enables you to assign and hold students responsible for generous amounts of work, but not to have to grade every item, yet still spot-check for completion and mastery. This can even be carried further: give pass/fail grades for completion on two of three assignments, and grade the third one closely (or a portion of it).

Some teachers even have students keep records of their own completion of assignments by requiring that the students keep a folder. Teachers have a method of marking the paper as completed on time, corrected, or whatever, and then all papers are kept in an appropriate section (e.g., vocabulary, grammar, culture, etc.) section of a notebook, and the notebook is evaluated on a random basis. Or from time to time, a "notebook quiz" is given, where answers from several different activities are requested, and the student is evaluated on his or her ability to produce the correct answer to demonstrate completion of the assignment. For example, choose three sentences at random, one from each of three assignments, and give five points for each correct answer. The only students hurt by this form of grading are those who consistently do careless work or who do not do the work at all.

MAKE EDITING A PART OF ANY PERFORMANCE

Let students know that their first effort, or only one effort, should never be their final one. The easiest way to do this is to require students to do an initial performance before their final one, and to make this a portion of their grade. I believe that real life usually gives us a chance to redo and improve our performances, and so I like to see this reflected in the classroom. When setting up a rubric, include a category such as "deadline met," "proofreading," or just "improved initial performance." If you give points, make it a small, yet significant portion; for example, if a written assignment is worth 50 points, it might break down like this:

10 pts.	Met assignment objectives (length, use of verb tenses, vocabulary, etc.)
15 pts.	Accuracy of verb endings, spelling, and so on
15 pts.	Understandability (or creativity)
10 pts.	Demonstrates editing (draft accompanies final product, met deadline for first draft)

Editing may be done by the teacher, and should use a self-correcting form similar to Figure 4.1 (p. 62) that holds the student responsible for finding the correction, rather than the teacher just writing the correct word and the student recopying it.

A variation on the above is to use a highlighter to mark mistakes, and give a grade the first time. Then, any student wishing a better grade may correct errors to earn half of the missing points back. For example, a student scoring 40 out of 50 points could increase his or her score to 45 by correcting everything.

Another option is to try using a "two strokes" system of assessment: On the first try, using the rubric, tell the student what grade that effort would receive if it were the final version. Give an initial grade (perhaps making it a small percent of the final grade, to avoid having tremendously sloppy initial efforts) along with suggestions for improvement. The second step is to challenge the student to improve his or her performance (usually by making improvement another portion of the final grade, as seen in the point system above). My daughter's college professors generally seem to use this system of having students submit a rough draft for general, holistic comments before closely grading the final draft. This method seems to provide a lot of opportunity for positive encouragement, while still allowing the final product to reflect the student's skills rather than the instructor's proofreading ability.

HOLD STUDENTS RESPONSIBLE FOR IMPROVEMENT

An important teaching tool that most of us use is the rough draft, but its use is generally limited to writing. Why not have a "rough draft" on an oral performance, or a "practice" listening activity, with feedback for students? There are several ways to do this that will streamline assessment. One way that I like for oral performances is called "Inside-Outside Circle" in most teaching strategy books. Have students prepare a skit, and perform it multiple times for classmates, by seating groups in a circle and pairing them. After performing for the other group, and getting feedback on pronunciation from their peers (e.g., "I think the rubric said you should tell two activities and you only did one."), they do a final "graded" performance for the teacher or the class. Not only do I have a better performance to grade, but students have had to perform the same situation multiple times instead of just once, better internalizing the structures, vocabulary, and pronunciation through repetition. Using Inside-Outside Circle for oral, written, or listening activities gets students involved in the evaluation procedure, and increases their familiarity with the objectives and criteria.

A variation on the above that holds students even more responsible is to make a portion of their grade depend on how perfect their classmates' performances are. For example, they must initial any rough draft that they have examined, and errors that survive in the final performance are their fault as well as their classmate's and influence their grade. Note that you need to set things up so that students can prove that they spotted the error and told their classmate to correct it; if the classmate didn't fix it, it does not count against the student who pointed out the correction.

I remember my daughter's frustration in a similar situation when she had a partner who just didn't care, and her grade went down as a result. Peer pressure is a great motivator for some students, but not all. Evaluation on peer editing should probably be limited to evaluating that it occurred, rather than that the desired results were achieved.

GIVE STUDENTS CHOICES

Students who are evaluated primarily on one skill that they don't have (or think they don't) quickly get discouraged. I cannot stress enough the importance of using variety in assessments, as well as in teaching strategies, or in making sure that the assessments reflect the teaching strategies used.

Giving choices can be as simple as allowing students to do any 5 of 8 essay questions, or answer 6 of 10 questions asked of them (saying "pass" for the others). Open-ended questions are another form of choice, allowing students more leeway in their responses: pick two famous people off the list provided, and describe them using two adjectives each; choose three times of a typical school day and for each tell what you would usually be doing then....

Several creative teachers have a tic-tac-toe approach to assessments that I compare to a Chinese restaurant menu, allowing students to choose one form of assessment from among several possibilities: "one from Column A, two from Columns B and C." For example, to display knowledge of vocabulary, a student could choose from among the following:

- ◆ Write a story correctly using at least 10 words from this chapter, underlining the words as they are used.

- ◆ Make a crossword puzzle with at least 10 words from this chapter, including clues and a key.

- ◆ Draw a storyboard for a story using at least 10 words from this chapter, and using the storyboard, tell the story to the teacher.

See Chapter 8 on alternative forms of assessment, or the topics discussed in Chapters 3 through 6 for some ideas on assessment options that can be offered.

Another variation on giving choices is particularly applicable to written or oral testing. Give students a list of questions they may be asked, and which they must learn to answer. Then, write each question on a piece of paper or an index card, and have students select a certain number of these at random to answer. This way, they are responsible for knowing answers to all the material, but are tested on a random few. For more advanced classes, perhaps a dialogue would be better than just a list of questions. Have them practice both asking and answering questions on several assigned topics, and then, in testing the student will speak on one of several situations (perhaps flipping a coin to determine which situation is used).

Consider allowing students to choose whether they wish to be tested alone, or with a partner, or in small groups. Each person should still receive an individual grade, but for some students, the thought of an exam (especially an oral one) one-on-one with a teacher is extremely frightening, and having a buddy along for moral support could be effective. Remember that brain research tells us that it is wise to re-create the learning situation when assessing. If this material was learned with a partner, or with the whole class interacting with the teacher, simply having a partner would allow students to more closely simulate the learning situation, and the student will have an easier time accessing what was learned. Especially if you have large classes, working with groups to test has other benefits—it somehow seems easier to manage 5 groups of 6 rather than 30 individuals in terms of movement, and the group tests could be spread out over several class periods as well.

KEEP RECORDS OF ASSESSMENTS

This is particularly effective for homework or behavioral assessment (such as speaking English in class). Print out a spreadsheet with all the students' names beside 10 columns (one for each day for a 2-week period). Check the box if the student has his or her homework done if the sheet is for keeping track of homework (or, perhaps, to save time, check only those who don't have homework). Do the same, in another color, or on another sheet, for behavior such as bad attitude, being disruptive, using English, criticizing classmates, or whatever characteristics you consider to be undesirable. This can easily be transferred later to a grade book, or check marks may be counted and deducted from a total and that percentage could form a portion of the student's final grade. For example, 5 check marks in 50 days would be 10% off, or a 5 points deducted from 50 possible points, which is 15% of the total number of points possible for the grading period.

APPLYING THE ABOVE RECOMMENDATIONS

Here is an example of a form of oral assessment that uses many of the streamlining methods described previously in this chapter, a good example of what can be done.

SELF-TAPING TO INCREASE FLUENCY

Students are told they must tape conversations outside class and turn these tapes in weekly as homework. They may use the school's language lab, a tape recorder of their own, or check out one of two departmental tape recorders. Discuss with them the benefits of taping to increase fluency. (The second year you do this, you will have favorable examples from the previous year to share.) They choose groups of two or three, each group providing three new blank cassette tapes labeled with their group name. One cassette will be used for only the first and last contribution of the year (the "souvenir" tape), and the other two will be used weekly (the "working" tapes). All students are given a product descriptor.

TAPE YOURSELF

Each week, you will record 15 minutes of conversation on any topic you want, on one of your group tapes.

You will need:

- A partner you will want to talk to and feel comfortable with (groups of 3 are OK) and whose schedule is similar to yours, if you want to do taping somewhere other than at school;
- Three 30-minutes cassette tapes for the group, labeled with your names; and
- A tape recorder of your own (optional).

You must:

- Begin the tape by saying your names and the date of the conversation.
- Completely fill one side of the tape, without any long pauses in the conversation. (If you run out of ideas, you may use two shorter conversations to fill the side, but must give your names and the date for each).
- Not use any language other than French.
- Speak unrehearsed, not using any written materials.
- Rewind the cassette to the beginning when you are finished taping.

You will not receive credit for the recording if:

- You use the wrong size tape;
- Your tape is not labeled;
- You do not say your names and the date;
- You do not rewind the tape to the beginning;
- You read conversations from the book instead of speaking freely;
- You use English on the tape (except people and place names);
- You do not fill one side of the tape; or
- You have too many long pauses.

Failure to do the above will result in you being asked to redo the tape, or in loss of credit.

Ideas for Topics

Any topic is OK! Suggestions:

- Places you have gone recently (vacations?)
- Family and friends
- Movies or TV shows
- Music or musicians
- Recent news
- Sports and/or teams
- Something you've read
- Things you like or don't like
- Something you plan to do

The first week, the group fills one side of the souvenir tape with free conversation, and the teacher collects and keeps these tapes until the end of the year, at which time the group records another conversation on the other side. Both the teacher and the students will listen to and compare the two samples, evaluating progress in things such as word count, length of answers, variety of topics, and ease of speaking (Figure 7.1). This tape will be an important record of their progress, and good to add to a student portfolio if desired.

Each week thereafter, the group will fill one side of one of the two working tapes with free conversation in the target language. There will always be one tape for the teacher to be assessing, and another for the students to use for recording.

To grade these tapes, the teacher must first check to make sure that they are completely filled, and then evaluate the contents. Listening to it all is impractical and unnecessary; just use the fast forward button to check the beginning, middle, and end. If two tape recorders are available, one tape can be listened to while fast-forwarding the other, saving additional time. The contents may be assessed in two ways: one way is to give a pass/fail credit for doing the tape, saving the assessment portion for the comparison of the first/last tape itself. A second way is to assign a certain number of points per tape, with failing to meet certain requirements involving a deduction of points or a request to redo the tape. Make sure that they know you mean it! After checking the tape, put a Post-It note or card with the evaluated tape with any comments on any glaring errors in word choice or usage, and a bit of praise or encouragement.

I erase the tapes, using a bulk tape eraser, before returning them so as to avoid students' just changing the date at the beginning and turning in a previously recorded tape. I also keep a note card with the topics discussed on each tape turned in to try to head off any lack of variety in their conversations. The students' enthusiasm for making these has been somewhat surprising.

The benefits of this activity are great: hours of extra practice speaking in the target language as well as increased confidence in their abilities to speak in a conversational situation.

FIGURE 7.1 SELF-EVALUATION

First Taping (Side A)

Topics from this taping:

Now choose THREE 10-second sections where you alone are speaking at the beginning, middle, and near the end of the tape. Count how many words you say in each 10-second section.

- A. Words per 10 seconds (from the beginning) = _____
- B. Words per 10 seconds (from the middle) = _____
- C. Words per 10 seconds (from near the end) = _____

FIRST FLUENCY: 2 × (A + B + C) = _____ Words per Minute

Last Taping (Side B)

Topics from this taping:

Now choose THREE 10-second sections where you alone are speaking at the beginning, middle, and near the end of the tape. Count how many words you say in each 10-second section.

- D. Words per 10 seconds (from the beginning) = _____
- E. Words per 10 seconds (from the middle) = _____
- F. Words per 10 seconds (from near the end) = _____

LAST FLUENCY: 2 × (D + E + F) = _____ Words per Minute

Circle your answers based on your feelings at the end of this semester:

My fluency	increased	didn't increase
The topics used	varied greatly	didn't vary
My sentences	got longer	stayed the same.
My partner(s)	was helpful	could have done more to help
I improved a lot	improved a little	did not improve
I thought it was easy	thought it somewhat easy	thought it was hard
I thought it was useful	thought it was somewhat useful	thought it was a waste of time
I thought it was interesting	thought it was okay	thought it was boring

List two things you learned while doing this tape:

1.

2.

Other comments:

8

ALTERNATIVE FORMS OF ASSESSMENT

Some forms of assessment involve testing several skills at once, working in concert. For this reason, they are also often referred to as "authentic" assessment because, as we know, when interacting with another person in a foreign language, we often use many skills at once. The most common examples of alternative assessment are the portfolio and the project, but you will find several others in this chapter as well.

K-W-L-U SHEETS

One of the simplest forms of alternative assessment that I find highly practical is a K-W-L-U sheet. We begin one as we begin a new unit, taking a sheet of paper and folding it in half and in half again in the same direction, so that, when the paper is opened, there are four sections across the page:

K	W	L	U

The first section we label "K" for "Know"; the second section is labeled "W" for "Want to Know"; and the third section is labeled L for "Learned"; and the fourth section is labeled "U" for "Used." The first day, we only use the K and W portions, as I give students the category (e.g., weekend activities, weather, famous speakers of the language, or whatever the unit topic is). In the "K" portion, they may write only in the target language, all the words they already know relating to this topic. As they do so, I walk around and look (gently correcting spelling or gender). I then have a good idea of what the students already are able to do. This is a great tool as it eliminates my spending time teaching things that they already seem to know, and it shows me how well my students have retained material taught (as I am not the only teacher that they have had for this language). It can serve students as well either as an opportunity to celebrate all that they remember or as a motivator as they see how little they know, and how much they need to learn. As students complete the "K" section, they also fill in the "W" section with all the words in that category that they cannot recall or haven't learned, and "Want" to know. At end of this activity, I like to give them an opportunity to "Roam around the Room" and look at their partners' papers; this can serve to jog their memories about aspects of the category they haven't thought of. For example, with sports, some students, on an individual basis, only think about team sports or those offered at the school, and by partnering will remember others such as ping-pong, sailing, and off-road biking.

At a several other times in the unit, we revisit this sheet, adding new material learned in the "L" column, with a "clean-up" day towards the end to handle words they wish to know that haven't been covered yet. I do not let them copy from the text onto the "L" portion, because if they need to do so, they haven't truly learned it yet.

As the final portion of this activity, either as homework or, sometimes, as their test over this material, in the "U" column, they must use this vocabulary, in logical sentences, to demonstrate their understanding of it. If the category was body parts, they must draw and label a body. If action verbs, they may write individual sentences, a letter, a story, or a picture for each verb in the "L" column. If I use this as a final assessment for the unit, I usually have them fold the "K" and "W" columns under the paper (or remove them), as the "W" column contains the "L" words in English.

We keep all these sheets for review purposes for our final exam. Student evaluations indicate that students view these as quite useful. These sheets are also great for students to share with parents at conference time.

PERFORMANCE PORTFOLIOS

Another highly useful assessment tool that may be shared with students and parents is a performance portfolio. A portfolio is more than a folder stuffed with student papers, audio- and/or videotapes, drawings, or other materials. It must be a purposeful collection of student work that tells the story of a stu-

dent's efforts, progress, or achievement in a given area over a period of time. In-
variably, proponents of performance assessment also advocate the use of student portfolios. There are two reasons usually given for this. The first is
dissatisfaction with the kind of information typically provided to students, parents, teachers, and members of the community about what students have
learned or are able to do. The second reason is that a well-designed portfolio
system can accomplish several important purposes: it can motivate students; it
can provide explicit examples to parents, teachers, and others of what students
know and are able to do; it allows students to chart their growth over time and
to self-assess their progress; and, it encourages students to engage in self-reflec-
tion. When designing a portfolio, consider these issues:

♦ What will it look like?

   There must be a physical (what documents are used and how they
   are stored) and a conceptual structure (work around a theme, e.g.,
   best work, celebration, showcase, representative, or chronological).

♦ What goes in?

   To decide what goes in the portfolio, numerous other questions need
   to be addressed: Who is the intended audience for the portfolios?
   What will this audience want to know about student learning? What
   kinds of evidence will best show student progress toward your iden-
   tified learning goals? Will the portfolio contain best work only, a progressive record of student growth, or both? If you want to show
   growth, include student work from various times during the period.
   If you want to show best learning, as for a job, have students choose
   what they consider to be their best effort.

♦ How and when should items be selected?

   Student participation in the selection process is critical, for this enables students to reflect on their work and monitor their progress.
   This is the key feature of using a portfolio as a performance assessment. Materials that are included should be dated and include an explanation for their inclusion, called a reflection sheet (otherwise,
   over time, students may forget why they included this item).

♦ How and when should portfolios be evaluated?

   Establish evaluation standards before the portfolio is begun. Portfolios are usually evaluated in terms of standards of excellence based
   on curriculum, or on growth demonstrated within an individual
   portfolio, rather than on comparisons made among different stu-

dents' portfolios. As for when, students should be asked to review their portfolio often. Teachers usually review them at the very least as a portion of a student's semester or final grade. As for parents and the community, consider holding a Portfolio Night. At this time, the parent(s) and children review student artifacts and reflections, affording a chance to see evidence of student growth firsthand, celebrate student progress (things they are proud of), and talk about areas needing more attention and effort, as well as what they are now currently exploring and what their goals are for this class.

Finally, remember that a portfolio is a process, not a destination. Good portfolios result from:

◆ Keeping the process simple;

◆ Including more than just written work;

◆ Asking students to explain and record why they chose each work sample;

◆ Maintaining a clear purpose; and

◆ Ensuring students have involvement and ownership.

PROJECTS

Projects, whether used as a final grade for a unit or in tandem with a written test, generally incorporate several skills, usually written and oral, with a uniquely creative aspect, and therefore need specific expectations and rubrics created for them. Students generally enjoy projects and appreciate knowing exactly what performance is expected, as well as how it will be evaluated. For this reason, it is a good idea to provide students with the project descriptor and the rubric at the same time. It is also a good idea to give students choices as to what sort of project they must do. Students generally have some sense of their learning style(s) and will select one that will be the most beneficial to them. This will result in increased enthusiasm, a sense of ownership on the part of the student, and a better project.

Examples of projects are:

◆ When doing clothing, to have students create a catalog page, and then order items from each other's pages;

◆ Getting a weather report off the Internet, drawing a map, and then doing a fake "broadcast";

- Read a book or story and create a mobile that shows aspects of the setting, characters, and plot, and explain your product; or,

- Incorporate the kinesthetic aspect by having students research (from foreign language Internet sources) and demonstrate something such as, hockey, ballet, lacrosse, bullfighting, engineering a subway or bridge, science discoveries, and so on.

GIVING CHOICES

Giving choices is one secret to getting good project results. Occasionally a project incorporates so much of a student's own personality that this provides enough options, but more often we must suggest several options in a sort of Chinese-restaurant-style format (one from Column A, two from Column B). Figure 8.1 (p. 114) is an example of this format.

Generally, the items in Figure 8.1 are assigned as homework, with students required to specify what type of activity they will do. Then, on the due date, the various products are displayed in the classroom and used as a learning-station activity: students are given a form to fill out as they view the various products. The form asks them to use the chapter vocabulary in various situations. For example, the audio- and videotapes can serve as a sort of "quiz" with students required to write down the words, and the flashcards can be a timed "race" to see who can name them fastest. Another important aspect of choice could be that of working alone, or as part of a group.

INCORPORATING TECHNOLOGY

Once you know what technology has to offer, it is easy to incorporate computer-room capabilities into projects you already use. Here are some examples:

- Have students create a school schedule using the Tables feature in a word-processing program in the target language—hour, subject, room, and teacher name should all be included.

- Use a word-processing program to create a trifold brochure, with different types of information on each portion. I have used this to have second-year students create a brochure on a famous French person they have researched (sections on life data, accomplishments, and influence, with a picture on the front and bibliography plus student name on the back) or a tourism brochure about the area where we live in (containing a list of activities, sites of interest, as well as directions on how to get here) as part of a career-oriented skills unit for a fourth-year class.

FIGURE 8.1 GIVING CHOICES

Using at least 20 vocabulary words from this chapter's vocabulary, do the following:

- ♦ Choose at least *one* of the following:
  - Design a crossword puzzle or a word search with clues in English and a key provided.
  - Use each of the vocabulary words in a sentence not found in the textbook (must be original).
  - Write a postcard.
  - Make an audiocassette in which you read the vocabulary word, pronouncing it correctly, followed by the English equivalent.

- ♦ And any *two* of the following:
  - Make flash cards with a colored picture on one side, and the vocabulary word on the other. Pictures may be original or cut out.
  - Make a poster, a collage, or hanging mobile with vocabulary words illustrated and labeled.
  - Draw a cartoon using vocabulary words as either dialogue or picture labels.
  - Write a story and read it on tape.
  - Make a board game using vocabulary from the chapter.
  - Write a song or rap (and perform it).
  - Make a scrapbook or booklet of pictures illustrating vocabulary, labeled correctly.
  - Make a video in which vocabulary is shown and the words are also spoken.

♦ Use a presentation program to have students create a menu, with pictures, or perhaps even expand it to include recipes, for a banquet to be held during Foreign Language Week. Another popular presentation program project is a series of five slides showing what students and their family/friend/pet likes or doesn't like. Presentation programs combine a visual with an auditory, as students must read aloud (and pronounce correctly) the words on the screen as they present it. To incorporate a written assignment, have students take notes as they view the presentation, and follow it up with a game the next day to see who remembers that Ana's favorite food was chocolate, for instance (an assessment that would test retention of the material presented the day before).

♦ My text series (*Discovering French*) has interactive CD-ROMs that accompany it, on which students may create a skit or a short play, recording their own voices as the dialogue. I am sure other series offer this possibility as well.

♦ Create a trivia search using a CD-ROM encyclopedia, or one of the web search sites available. I use TrackStar (http://scrtec.org/track/tracks) and can use one already created there, or modify one for my needs, or create my own.

♦ Use word processing or desktop publishing software to create a newsletter for the class (e.g., have the seniors write a will to the underclassmen or study tips). This could also be something sent home to parents. Or, the newsletter could be a fictional one showing students' research on a particular time period, such as a medieval newspaper complete with adds for new products, laws, fashions, as well as reports on events.

♦ Use Daedalus or similar conferencing systems for an electronic class "debate." Post a question (or more) to which students reply. All students see each other's answers, and type and post responses, leaving the teacher free to circulate and correct errors about to be made. Absent students can participate later, and students may come back the next day and finish a discussion that interested them. If you don't own such a program, check FLTEACH archives for "online message board" addresses and Internet Web sites to which you can take students and have them post responses to questions, but they will not get immediate responses.

ASSESSING BEHAVIORS

Some schools use behavioral assessment schoolwide and assign it a substantial percentage of a student grade. More often, behavioral rubrics are used as a portion of a grade on a project, especially if needed for disciplinary reasons such as to make sure students complete work in an orderly fashion, on time, or with every student contributing in proportion to their abilities. Again, these rubrics, if they are to be used, should be shared with students before beginning the assignment.

ASSESSING INDIVIDUAL RESPONSIBILITY

Figure 8.2 is a sample behavioral assessment rubric to give students. It really helps students if they can see a written description of an active learner. Make a spread chart for each student in a class with 10 columns for recording a grade from 1 to 10. The total will add up to 100 points, and instantly convert to a percentage. On any random day throughout a grading period, evaluate several students (take the number of students in your class times 10, divided by the number of days in the grading period to get the number you need to evaluate per day).

FIGURE 8.2 DAILY PERFORMANCE GRADE

9–10 Exceeds the standard	Helps facilitate classroom activity. Demonstrates engaged, active learning throughout the class period. Makes consistently strong contributions to the classroom activity.
8 Meets the standard	Participates in a generally constructive way. Demonstrates engaged, active learning through part of the class period. Makes strong contributions to the classroom activity.
7 Approaches the standard	Has little negative or positive effect on the class and its progress. May be grappling with the ideas addressed in class but shows little evidence of learning. Prepares, but makes little contribution to the classroom activity.
5-6 Falls below the standard	Has more of a negative effect on the class than positive. Required work or preparation incomplete. Disruptive behavior makes learning difficult for others. Refuses to stay on task.
0 Fails to meet standard	Sent out of class or truant. Sleeps.

If working in teams, you may also want to assess whether team members demonstrated individual responsibility by listening to others, helping teammates, doing an equal share of the work, or using praise and encouragement instead of "put downs."

Figure 8.3 is a sample rubric for listening skills.

FIGURE 8.3 RUBRIC FOR LISTENING SKILLS

---

4 pts.	The student actively listens to and values the opinions of others.
3 pts.	The student actively listens, but it is not evident that he/she values the opinions of others.
2 pts.	The student listens to but does not value the opinions of others, or the student values the opinions of others but does not listen to them.
0 pts.	The student does not listen to and does not value the opinions of others.

USING RUBRICS TO ASSESS TEAM RESPONSIBILITY

While doing a project, you may want to assess team responsibility by observing such behaviors as whether the team is solving its problems itself, asking each other before asking the teacher, helping other teams, or using its "quiet voice," a volume heard by teammates, but not by other teams. Figure 8.4 is a sample rubric for problem-solving skills.

FIGURE 8.4 RUBRIC FOR PROBLEM-SOLVING SKILLS

---

4 pts.	The team tries to solve its problems by itself, without seeking outside help.
3 pts.	The team seldom solves its problems as a team and asks classmates or the teacher for help.
2 pts.	The team seldom solves its problems and gives up easily.
0 pts.	The team never attempts to solve its problems and gives up readily.

SELF-ASSESSMENT

Teams and individuals may also be asked to assess themselves. Many studies show that this is a valid and reliable measure of language proficiency. In fact, it has been argued that greater quality of learning may be ensured by putting control over the learning in the place where it must occur—namely, in the mind of the learner. Knowing that they will have to answer questions about their performance makes students very self-aware and most respond quite favorably.

Most often, self-assessment is done at the end of an assignment. A fun way to ask team to assess themselves according to their contribution to the product is to give them an imaginary dollar, franc, peso, and mark amount, and ask how much each should be "paid" based on their amount of work. Students are generally fairly honest in evaluating this, and I find that the students in a group, even when their evaluation is done separately from the other group members, generally agree as to the value of everyone's contribution.

For individual assessment, I find that an open-ended form, such as that in Figure 8.5, generates more introspection than one that provides boxes to check.

FIGURE 8.5 AN OPEN-ENDED SELF-ASSESSMENT FORM

◆ How many hours did you spend working on this project?

◆ To what portion of the project did you contribute most?

◆ What was the most enjoyable part of this project?

◆ What did you learn by doing this project?

◆ What might you do differently next time?

◆ What is a possible follow-up on this topic that you might do in the future?

USING MENTORING IN THE CLASSROOM

Pairing students with a peer mentor is also a wonderful way to assure that learning will take place for both of them. Al Bode of Charles City, Iowa and winner of the prestigious 2000 Charles F. Martin Award for teaching, has allowed me to present this wonderful idea in this book. He has experimented for the past four years with the use of student-mentors in the first and second-year classes. For the past 20 years or so, Mr. Bode, as so many of us have, had attempted to accommodate two or more levels of students in a single classroom, finding that, "while it seemed to benefit the underclasspersons and increased their skills through having helpful models and encouraging older students, the advanced levels did not always gain to the degree expected. Responsibility and self-reliance were not always present." His creative solution was to create a mentor program in which third-year and fourth-year students who cannot fit in a Spanish class due to crowded schedules can mentor first- and second-year students, respectively. He states that that the mentoring program

> free[s] me to circulate among groups during oral drills and written drills conducted by the mentors...to reach those having difficulties faster and diagnos[e] the problems, and I don't have to get on a student's case for inaction because peer pressure and the desire to succeed in the mentor's eyes govern the efforts of underclasspersons. Advanced students can pre-check written tests and prep students for oral testing. They can contribute all kinds of artwork. They can monitor drill and enrichment work programs and achievement through computer software. And most interesting of all is the ability of some of those who had difficulty at the outset of first year to become excellent mentors and taskmasters for similar students two years later! Students choose to mentor and we discuss it; very few would rather switch to regular advanced classes if schedule permits at trimester break, but it is their choice, following individual trimester evaluations. Some students try a mixture purposely and find each class offers unique opportunities. The most important consideration is continued growth and confidence in acquiring another culture and language.

Students model the language, drill students, assist them in writing skills, and monitor progress on computer-assisted work. They also have other requisites that they must complete that pertain to third- or fourth-year Spanish. Mr. Bode says, "They claim that they learn the material much more than when they originally encountered it because they are now 'teaching' it!" This corresponds with all the research on learning strategies to employ to increase retention.

He has developed rubrics to evaluate mentor work, as well as "more in-depth" sessions with mentors only to assist them in working with their groups. On pages 120 through 123 are the rubrics that Mr. Bode used for his "Mentoring for the 1999–2000 School Year" program.

MENTOR'S RESPONSIBILITIES

♦ Modeling

Mentors are expected to be worthy models for lower-level students. This includes being on time for class, classroom care, and behavior within the classroom, and knowing materials and units studied very well. With this responsibility comes the mandate that uncertainties in classroom management or grammatical/pronunciation accuracy should be immediately resolved by a mentor-teacher cooperative conference.

♦ Roll-Taking

Mentors are responsible for selecting primary and secondary roll-takers for each class. The primary roll-taking function should rotate each trimester and the secondary (back-up) roll-takers should always be ready to assume this function when the primary roll-taker is absent. Record should be timely and accurate. Above all, mentors need to stress to lower-level students the necessity for *signing in themselves* each day.

♦ Tutoring

Students with incomplete learning behavior due to illness, extended absences, or inadequate study habits may require individual help. Mentors will be required to keep progress records for these students.

♦ Drill

Mentors will be extensively involved in conducting drills in the classroom. These may include the following classifications:

• Oral drill using flash card and/or stimuli. Mentors may use classroom materials or be required to create copies as necessity dictates. Oral drill by flash cards may be conducted in large group (or combined group), small group (assigned group), or individual response modes. Mentors may use sheets with written questions as stimuli or use a common sheet provided all students. Careful listening is required of mentors in drilling other students. Students may also use blackboard stimuli for eliciting responses.

• Mentors will keep careful records of daily progress of the students in their groups. Procedures will be explained during second week orientation.

- As class-involvement drills such as challenge, lotería, community quiz and other non-flash card drills are employed, mentors are expected to lead or take part in conducting these exercises. Overall, mentors should be prepared to be involved in each class hour and not use class time as a study hall for other classes.

Other Considerations

♦ Grading

Grading will be through a rubric that measures the mentor's in-class involvement, carefulness, and accuracy of work produced individually and by designated small group, and overall benefit to lower-level students demonstrated by their understanding and achievement under mentored guidance.

♦ Limitations

A maximum of four students per mentor will be sought in each of four L-1 sections and two L-2 classes. Responsibilities listed above are not an all-inclusive list of standard duties to be performed by mentors.

Criteria for Evaluation: L-2 (Student Mentor)

5. Executes routine (daily) tasks promptly and efficiently.

6. Accepts corrections as educational requisites for improvement.

7. Brings all necessary materials to class.

8. Efficiently uses class hour to study the unit, without wasting time.

9. Makes continual and solid effort to learn Spanish.

RUBRIC #1: "MENTORING" EN LA CLASE:
USING THE TARGET LANGUAGE

Mentor _____   Hour _____

	Excellent	*Acceptable*	*Poor*
Use of Spanish before & after class period:	Student always speaks Spanish once inside the classroom. 5	Student uses some Spanish in classroom, but prefers to just not talk. 4 3	Student uses English, whispers to talk in English, or says nothing. 2 1 0
Activities within the classroom and required coursework:	Student always speaks Spanish with partner(s). Uses Spanish beyond immediate coursework to expand conversation. 10 9	Student mostly speaks Spanish, resorts to some English when faced with difficulties. Only discusses questions given. 8 7 6	Student frequently uses English both for activity and conversing of thins not related to coursework being completed. 5 4 3 2 1 0
Classtime participation:	Student is focused during class. Participates freely in Spanish. Asks in Spanish to understand; doesn't give up when attempting something in Spanish (sees it through). 10 9	Student is fairly focused in class. Occasionally participates in Spanish. Attempts to ask questions in Spanish; give up when cannot think of exact Spanish words. 8 7 6	Student is not focused in class. Only participates in class when called on. Never makes an attempt to ask questions in Spanish. 5 4 3 2 1 0

Contributed by Al Bode

RUBRIC #2: "MENTORING" EN LA CLASE: STUDENT LEVEL OF RESPONSIBILITY IN GROUP WORK, ACTIVITIES, AND DRILLS

Mentor _____   Hour _____

	Excellent	*Acceptable*	*Poor*
Use of Spanish before & after class period:	Mentor always speaks Spanish once inside the classroom. 5	Mentor uses some Spanish in classroom, but prefers to just not talk. 4 3	Mentor uses English, whispers to talk in English, or says nothing. 2 1 0
Activities within the classroom and required coursework:	Mentor is responsible when appointed for roll-taking, keeping records of student & group progress and knowing the units in advance. 10 9	Mentor is somewhat responsible, but needs reminders occasionally to complete daily tasks in recording progress and roll-taking functions. 8 7 6	Mentor needs frequent reminders and assistance in completing record-keeping tasks. 5 4 3 2 1 0
Classtime leadership:	Mentor is focused during class. Leads drills freely in Spanish. Accepts challenge of different students in group. Volunteers to lead activities. Maintains positive rapport with group. 10 9	Mentor is fairly focused in class. Usually leads drills & activities in Spanish. Is an adequate leader. Often able to lead only own group. Group usually performs at adequate level. 8 7 6	Mentor lacks constant focus in class. Only accepts leadership in class when called on to do so. Group harmony is often lacking regardless of personnel therein. 5 4 3 2 1 0

Contributed by Al Bode

MIND MAPS AND POWER PICTURES

Based upon an idea found in *Learning and Memory: The Brain in Action* by Marilee Sprenger, I created an assignment for third-year students to create a self-portrait using a human body with each part labeled as follows:

♦ Head—my thoughts

♦ Eye—Something I have seen

♦ Other eye—something I'd like to see

♦ Ear—something I have heard

♦ Arm—one of my talents

♦ Heart—a person and a thing I like

♦ Mouth—something I want to say

♦ Leg—somewhere I have gone

♦ Other leg—somewhere I'd like to go

♦ Foot—something I don't like

On the day your person is due, you will be paired with another student. You must ask at least three questions about the person, and answer three questions about yours.

Here are the rubrics:

An A person:	A B person	A C person	Unacceptable (F)
• Person is neatly drawn • Each of the 10 body parts are explained • No errors in grammar • Creative	• Is neatly drawn • All 10 well explained error-free	• A stick figure explained very briefly • Has one or two errors	• Incompletely labeled (less than 10 parts) • Has more than two errors • Assignment not done or late
An A oral grade:	A B oral grade:	A C oral grade:	Unacceptable (F)
• Ask and answer 3 ?s • Detailed answers (more than is basically required) • Flawless grammar	• Ask and answer 3 ?s • Briefly answers question • No errors in speaking	• Ask and answer 3 ?s • Answers questions with hesitation • One or two errors in speaking	• Less than 3 questions • Inability to answer any questions • More than two errors

ADDITIONAL EXAMPLES PROVIDED
BY FOREIGN LANGUAGE TEACHERS

Le Sac des Vêtements (Sack of Clothing) (p. 126) and *Si j'allais… (If I went…)* (p. 127), were contributed by Sandra Howard, teacher at Marin Catholic High School, Kentfield, CA.

Hier, Aujourd'hui, et Demain (Yesterday, Today, and Tomorrow) consists of a set of lesson plans (p. 128), instructions (p. 131), and rubrics (p. 134) for making and dressing a cute sock doll as well as writing a descriptive essay. It was contributed by Rebecca Peters, White Plains Middle School for the Humanities at Eastview, White Plains, NY.

Le Sac des Vêtements
(Sack of Clothing)

You will create a shopping bag, or you may use a real shopping bag. The paper must be in the shape of a sack. You may not use binder paper. Make sure it is big enough for all your articles.

On the sack you will glue or draw and color 7 different clothing items. You must describe each article of clothing in a complete sentence. Use the new vocabulary on page _____ as well as colors. Don't keep repeating the same words! Some sample sentences:

♦ La robe rouge coûte $100; elle est chère.

♦ J'aime bien le maillot vert; il est très à la mode.

♦ Les chaussures marron ne sont pas moches; elles sont très jolies.

♦ Je pense que la cravate noire et blanche est démodée.

Grading

Nom _____

Directions (3)   _____

Verbes (7)   _____

Adjectifs (7) _____

Variété de vocabulaire (3) _____

Présentation (5)_____

TOTAL: 25 points possible_____

SI J'ALLAIS...
(IF I WENT...)

Make a poster with at least 10 sentences in the conditional tense. You must use 10 different verbs. Remember that you're in French III. Don't give me French I sentences! You must have at least 5 pictures of the place you visit or activities you do there. They may be photos, cutouts from a magazine or travel brochure, or personal drawings. The title of the poster will be "Si j'allais + *name of the place*." Check with me for the proper French spelling of the place and for the correct preposition preceding the place.

These posters will be displayed in class, so make sure they are visually appealing and neat.

Grades will be based on the following:

10 pts.	Verbs
5 pts.	General grammar and structure
5 pts.	Neatness and visual appeal
TOTAL:	20 points

HIER, AUJOURD'HUI, ET DEMAIN
(YESTERDAY, TODAY, AND TOMORROW)

Lesson Plan

French 8 (periods 4 and 8)

Week of January 10, 2000—projects due Tuesday, January 18, 2000

Standards	• Students will develop cross-cultural skills and understanding • Students will read, write, listen, and speak for communication in the LOTE
Objectives	• Students will be able to read and follow directions • Students will be able to write using the past, present, and immediate future tenses • Students will be able to read for comprehension
Skills	• Sewing • Reading • Writing
Performance Objectives	• Students will be able to create a doll per the step-by-step directions they will be given in French • Students will be able to write a descriptive essay about clothing using the past, present, and future tenses • Students will be able to read descriptions of each doll and match the dolls to the descriptions.
Essential Vocabulary	• Sewing • Clothing • Directions (imperatives)
Differentiated Learning Activities	Multisensory learning. Specific learning modalities including oral presentation, written expression, and reading and listening skills will be addressed throughout the assignment allowing each student to use his or her preferred modality while strengthening the others.

Collaboration with Inclusion Teacher	• Extended time for project • Where necessary, writing template provided
Assessment	• Essay • Matching activity
Process	• Explain project in English • Pre-teach vocabulary • Give students direction sheets (remind them to check off as they complete each step and to have me sign at the end) • Students will begin process of sewing per directions • Once dolls are completed, they will have to dress them with at least five articles of clothing or accessories • Essays need to be three paragraphs of at least five sentences each. The first paragraph will introduce the doll and describe what the doll was wearing yesterday and why. The second paragraph will detail what the doll is wearing today (how the doll is dressed) and the third paragraph will describe what the doll will wear tomorrow. • Dolls and rough drafts will be collected on Tuesday, January 18. • Drafts will be returned to students on Wednesday, January 19. • Final drafts due on Friday, January 21. • On Monday, January 24, students will present their dolls to the class and describe what they are wearing. • On Tuesday, January 25, students will be handed descriptions of each doll (in French). The dolls will be displayed throughout the room and each doll will have a number. Students will read the descriptions and match the doll's number to each.
Homework	• Students should begin their essay. Rough draft and dolls are due Tuesday, January 18 and final draft will be due Friday, January 21.

Resources/Materials	• Glue (hot and regular)
	• Material
	• Needles
	• Index cards
	• Pencils
	• Plastic bags (gallon size)
	• Plastic eyes
	• Polyester stuffing
	• Ribbon
	• Rulers
	• Scissors
	• Socks
	• String
	• Thread
	• Yarn
	• Direction sheets
Hints	• Ask teachers, parents, or local craft shops for fabric and craft remnants
	• Give each student a plastic freezer bag in which he or she may keep all of his or her supplies. Each bag should be labeled with a name. This will help students stay organized and be responsible for their own materials.
	• Give each student a 3×5 card with a needle poked through it. Each student will have his or her own needle. Each student should label the card with his or her name and place the card inside the bag. Instruct each student to replace the needle in the card each time it is not in use. This will help prevent lost needles. In the interest of safety, students *should not* share needles.

STUDENT DIRECTIONS

(Note: Translation done by the author
of this book and is not part of handout!)

Vous allez avoir besoin de:
(You will need:)

- Une chaussette
- Une règle
- Un crayon
- Des ciseaux
- Le fil
- Une aiguille
- La bourre (en polyester)
- La ficelle
- Des feutres
- Le ruban
- Le tissu
- La colle

(One sock, a ruler, a pencil, some scissors, thread, a needle, polyester stuffing, twine, some felt tip markers, ribbon, fabric, and glue.)

Cochez (✔) quand vous avez fini chaque travail.
(Check each step when finished.)

_____ 1. Mettez la chaussette à l'envers.

   (Turn sock inside out.)

_____ 2. Pour faire les bras: mesurez environ 5 centimètres du bout. Dessinez une ligne.

   (To make arms, measure about 5 centimeters from the end, and draw a line.)

_____ 3. Marquez au milieu et faites un "T" en dessinant une ligne de la première ligne au bout de la chaussette.

   (Mark the middle and make a "T" by drawing a line from the first line to the end of the sock.)

_____ 4. Coupez les deux lignes.
(Cut both lines.)

_____ 5. Cousez les bords.
(Sew the raw edges together on each piece. You will have two arms.)

_____ 6. Quand vous avez fini, tournez à l'endroit et remplissez avec la bourre.
(Turn right-side out and stuff.)

_____ 7. Cousez au quatrième bord. Gardez les bras jusqu'à plus tard.
(Sew the remaining edge.)

_____ 8. Maintenant, retournez à la chaussette. Au nouveau bout, marquez le milieu et dessinez une ligne de 6 ou 7 centimetres.
(Go back to the sock. Mark the middle and draw a 6- or 7-centimeter line.)

_____ 9. Coupez la ligne.
(Cut along that line.)

_____ 10. Pour faire les jambes, cousez aux bords.
(To make legs, sew the raw edges together.)

_____ 11. Ensuite, tournez la chaussette à l'endroit.
(Turn the sock right-side out.)

_____ 12. Remplissez la chaussette avec la bourre jusqu'à la ligne naturelle en haut de la chaussette.
(Fill the sock with stuffing up to the line where the sock meets the ribbed cuff.)

_____ 13. Faites un noeud avec la ficelle autour de la ligne naturelle pour fermer la chaussette.
(Make a knot with the twine around the line to close off the sock. This is the body.)

_____ 14. Pour faire la tête, faites un autre noeud 7 ou 8 centimètres au-dessous du premier noeud. (Ce nouveau noeud est le cou.)
(To make a head, make another knot with string 7 or 8 centimeters below the first knot. (This makes the head.))

_____ 15. Cousez les bras au corps.
(Sew the arms to the body.)

Maintenant, votre poupée est finie. Ensuite, il faut faire les vêtements. Il faut avoir au moins cinq choses.
(Now your doll is finished. Next, you must make clothing. Make at least five items.)

_____ 16.   Décrivez les 5 vêtements ou accessoires ici:

(Describe the five items here:)

_____

_____

_____

_____

_____

Après avoir fini, écrivez une petite histoire. Il faut avoir:

_____ 5 phrases au passé composé (*Qu'est-ce qu'il/elle a porté hier?*)

_____ 5 phrases au présent (*Comment s'habille-t-il/elle aujourd'hui?*)

_____ 5 phrases au futur (*Qu'est-ce qu'il/elle va porter demain?* HINT: *Employez aller plus l'imfinitif.*)

(Now, write a little story, with 5 sentences in past tense, 5 in present, and 5 in future.)

_____ 17.   Donnez votre papier au prof et elle va le corriger.
             (Give your paper to the teacher for correction.)

_____ 18.   Tapez à machine votre histoire.
             (Now type your story and print it.)

_____ 19.   Donnez l'histoire et la poupée au prof.
             (Give your story and doll to the teacher.)

Signature du prof

Contributed by Rebecca Peters

RUBRIC FOR HIER, AUJOURD'HUI, ET DEMAIN

Nom: _____

The following project will count as a project grade and as a test grade for the second quarter.

♦ Create a doll according to the directions. Be sure to check off each step and get the paper signed by the teacher to hand in with your project. *Counts as Project Grade*

♦ Write a three-paragraph essay. Each paragraph should have at least five sentences and five articles of clothing or accessories. The first paragraph should use the past tense (what the doll wore yesterday), the second paragraph should use present tense (what the doll is currently wearing), and the third paragraph should be in the future tense (what the doll will be wearing tomorrow). *Counts as Project Grade*

♦ Present your doll to the class and be able to describe its outfit. *Counts as Two Classwork Grades*

♦ Read descriptions of others' dolls and match the descriptions to the doll. *Counts as Test Grade*

The following rubric will be used to score your written project.

	Superior Work	Demonstrates Competence	Suggests Competence	Suggests Incompetence	Incompetence
Organization	Well organized and well written. Exhibits a logical and coherent sequence of events throughout. All directions followed. Typed. 20	Fairly well organized. Connections are implied with few irrelevancies. Most directions followed. Typed. 12	A bit unorganized. Connections may be unclear with some irrelevancies. Directions not followed. Handwritten neatly. 8	Not well organized. Some statements irrelevant to the task. Directions not followed. Unclearly handwritten. 4	Not at all organized. Directions not followed. 0

	Superior Work	*Demonstrates Competence*	*Suggests Competence*	*Suggests Incompetence*	*Incompetence*
Comprehensibility	Completely appropriate and comprehensible to a native speaker with no knowledge of English. **20**	Appropriate and comprehensible in most parts to a native speaker. **12**	Most elements are appropriate and comprehensible to a native speaker with some knowledge of English. **8**	Ideas are poorly expressed but still comprehensible for a native speaker with some knowledge of English. **4**	Incomprehensible. **0**
Structure	Uses accents and makes few spelling errors. High degree of subject/verb/adjective agreement. **20**	In general, structure is good. Few spelling errors. Some control of subject/verb/adjective agreement. **12**	More than a few errors which hinder overall achievement and comprehensibility. **8**	Many errors in structure, accents and other basic errors which impede overall comprehensibility of the assignment. **4**	
Vocabulary/Grammar	Uses required vocabulary as well as incorporating a variety of old vocabulary and structure. Tense appropriate. **20**	Good use of new vocabulary and expressions. Limited incorporation of old vocabulary. Tense appropriate. **12**	Relies on a basic vocabulary. **8**	Errors in limited vocabulary and tense. **4**	Complete lack of comprehensible vocabulary. **0**

	Superior Work	Demonstrates Competence	Suggests Competence	Suggests Incompetence	Incompetence
Doll	Completed per directions and turned in on time. **20**	Completed per directions but turned in one (1) day late. **12**	Partially completed or two (2) or more days late. **8**		Incomplete **0**

The following rubric will be used to score your oral project.

	Superior Work	Demonstrates Competence	Suggests Competence	Suggests Incompetence	Incompetence
Fluency	Eagerly initiates speech, utilizing appropriate attention getting devices. Speaks spontaneously. **20**	Is willing to initiate speech, utilizing appropriate devices. Speaks evenly. **12**	Speaks hesitantly. **8**	Speech is halting. **4**	No utterances. **0**
Comprehensibility	Completely appropriate and comprehensible to a native speaker with no knowledge of English. **20**	Appropriate and comprehensible in most parts to a native speaker. **12**	Most elements are appropriate and comprehensible to a native speaker with some knowledge of English. **8**	Ideas are poorly expressed but still comprehensible for a native speaker with some knowledge of English. **4**	Incomprehensible. **0**

	Superior Work	Demonstrates Competence	Suggests Competence	Suggests Incompetence	Incompetence
Pronunciation	Speaks clearly and imitates accurate pronunciation. **20**	Speaks clearly and attempts accurate pronunciation. **12**	Speech is comprehensible in spit of mispronunciation. **8**	Mispronunciation impedes comprehensibility. **4**	Incomprehensible **0**
Vocabulary/Grammar	Uses required vocabulary as well as incorporating a variety of old vocabulary and structure. Tense appropriate. **20**	Good use of new vocabulary and expressions. Limited incorporation of old vocabulary. Tense appropriate. **12**	Relies on a basic vocabulary. **8**	Errors in limited vocabulary and tense. **4**	Complete lack of comprehensible vocabulary. **0**
Culture	Almost always uses/interprets cultural manifestations appropriate to the task (gestures, proximity, etc.) **20**	Frequently uses/interprets cultural manifestations appropriate to the task (gestures, proximity, etc.) **12**	Sometimes uses/interprets cultural manifestations appropriate to the task (gestures, proximity, etc.) **8**	Rarely uses/interprets cultural manifestations appropriate to the task. **4**	Has no concept of cultural manifestations appropriate to the task (gestures, proximity, etc.) **0**

And here is an example of a "A" student essay to go with the finished project:

Je vous présente Chantal.

Hier elle a fait du camping avec ses amis, donc, elle a porté des jeans et un tee-shirt rouge. Elle a porté des bottes avec l'ensemble. Hier soir, quand il faisait froid, elle a mis un pull jaune.

Aujourd'hui, elle va à l'église. Chantal porte une jupe qui a des fleurs et une veste bleue. Elle met un foulard jaune pour être chic. Elle porte aussi un chapeau noir avec un ruban blanc.

Demain, elle va retourner à l'école. Elle va porter une jupe verte et bleue foncé avec un chemisier blanc. Elle va mettre des chaussettes blanches avec des chaussures noires. S'il va faire froid, elle va mettre sa veste verte. Elle veut s'habiller bien pour aller à l'école!

Contributed by Rebecca Peters

BIBLIOGRAPHY

ARTICLES

Paulus, L. (March 1998). Watch them SOAR: Student oral assessment redefined. *Hispania, 81,* 146–152.

Schneider, P. (1993). Developing fluency with pair taping. *JALT Journal, 15*(1), 55–62.

Wiggins, G. (1990). *The case for authentic assessment.* ERIC Digest. (ED328611)

Wiggins, G. (1990) *Toward more instructionally-appropriate and effective testing: Authentic assessment.* Los Angeles, CA: Center for Research on Evaluation, Standards, and Student Testing (UCLA).

BOOKS

Blaz, D. (1999). *Foreign language teacher's guide to active learning.* Larchmont, NY: Eye on Education.

Herman, J. L., Aschbacher, P. R., & Winters, L. (1992). *A practical guide to alternative assessment.* Alexandria, VA: Association for Supervision and Curriculum Development.

Krashen, S. D., & Terrell, T. D. (1983). *The natural approach: Language acquisition in the classroom.* San Francisco, CA: Alemany.

Mislevy, R. J. (1989). *Foundations of a new test theory.* Princeton, NJ: Educational Testing Service.

Resnick, L. B., & Resnick, D. P. (1989). *Assessing the thinking curriculum: New tools for educational reform.* Pittsburgh, PA: Learning Research and Development Center, University of Pittsburgh and Carnegie Mellon University.

Sousa, D. A. (1995). *How the brain learns.* Reston, VA: National Association of Secondary School Principals.

Sprenger, M. (1999). *Learning and memory: The brain in action.* Alexandria, VA: Association for Supervision and Curriculum Development.

Stiggins, R.J. (1996). *Student-centered classroom assessment* (2nd ed.). Columbus, OH: Macmillan.

Stiggins, R. J., Webb, L. D., Lange, J., McGregor, S., & Cotton, S. (1997). *Multiple assessment of student progress.* Reston, VA: National Association of Secondary School Principals.

Sweet, D., & Zimmermann, J. (Eds.) (1992). *Performance assessment.* Washington, DC: Office of Educational Research and Improvement (ED).

139

INTERNET

FL-TEACH archives: http://listserv.acsu.buffalo.edu/archives/flteach.html and use the Search for a wealth of ideas for assessments and projects of different types.

Notes

Notes

Notes

Notes

Notes

Notes

Notes

Notes